Water from an Ancient Well

Celtic Spirituality for Modern Life

Water from an Ancient Well

Celtic Spirituality for Modern Life

Kenneth McIntosh

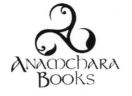

Anamchara Books

Water from an Ancient Well

Anamchara Books
Vestal, NY 13850
www.anamcharabooks.com

9 8 7 6 5 4 3

ISBN: 978-1-933630-98-4
ebook ISBN: 978-1-933630-99-1

Library of Congress Control Number 2011907336

Author: Kenneth McIntosh

Cover design by Russell Richardson.
Interior design by Camden Flath.
Printed in the United States of America.

Contents

Introduction
Reading This Book

Like a Celtic knot, this book is meant to be enjoyed in a nonlinear fashion: you don't need to read the whole volume in sequential order, since each chapter is an independent essay. Feel free to glance at the table of contents and then begin wherever you wish.

These chapters contain three aspects; the medium is the message, for three was the sacred number of the ancient Celts. First, true to the Celtic love of tales, each chapter has stories; some of these are contemporary, others ancient. Second, each chapter contains an examination of theology and history; the ancient scholar-saints would surely approve. And third, each chapter offers modern applications drawn from the theology and thinking of the past.

This book is not meant to present doctrine or a systematic theology. It does not claim to be the "right" way to approach Christianity. And it certainly does not set itself up as an argument against more traditional forms of Christianity. None of that would be in the spirit of Celtic Christianity.

The Celtic Christians were a theologically diverse group: when any two had a conversation, they could argue three different points of view! Many Gaelic churches affirmed women's equality, for instance, but some island monasteries forbade women from even stepping ashore. Some Celtic theologians warned of damnation for anyone outside the church, while others believed all humankind would be saved.

And yet for the most part, the Christian Celts tended to look at the world from a "both-and" perspective rather than an "either-or" one. They did not see their pagan ancestors' beliefs as a threat to their newer ones; instead, one complimented and illuminated the other. They believed God's light shone in all humans, and as a result, they were able to live comfortably side by side with people of varying beliefs.

Building on the ancient Celts' example of tolerance and open-mindedness, I have intentionally tried not to take a stand when it comes to choosing whether ancient theology and practices are "better" than modern ones. Undoubtedly, my personal preferences will show through in places, since my own story is part of this book, but I have done my best merely to examine the history that helps us understand how modern Christianity got where it is today from where it once was in the days and land of the ancient Celts—and to suggest that those older ways, while not perfect, still have something to offer us in the twenty-first century.

May the Divine Spirit allow you to find living water within these pages.

Deep peace of the running wave to you.
Deep peace of the flowing air to you.
Deep peace of the quiet Earth to you.
Deep peace of the sleeping stones to you.
Deep peace of the stars to you.
Deep peace of the Son of Peace to you.

1
SEEKING ANCIENT WELLS
THE CELTS AND THEIR WORLD

"Let anyone who is thirsty come to me and drink!"
—Jesus

This is what the LORD says:
"Stand at the crossroads and look;
ask for the ancient paths,
ask where the good way is, and walk in it,
and you will find rest for your souls."
—Jeremiah 6:16

I like to begin a new writing project with an appropriate ceremony, so this morning I took down from my office shelf a small plastic container filled with water labeled "St. Non's." The Earth is rich with water, some 326 million trillion gallons of it, but the liquid in this vial is special: I poured it from a Welsh sacred well, toted it in my backpack for weeks, and then checked it onto a flight to America. Now, I pour that water into a champagne flute and take a swallow. Ahh . . .

It tastes wonderful. But the natural qualities of a drink of water aren't what make me savor this liquid so much. Each drop is infused with legend.

The tale begins bitterly when a Welsh chieftain violated a young woman named Non. She struggled through the pregnancy that resulted, but when her son David was born, a spring burst miraculously from the ground. The waters met her practical needs, but drinking from the well also healed the young woman's broken spirit.

Since that year, 520 CE, pilgrims to St. Non's Well have claimed that its waters heal diseases of the eyes and bones. Even more miraculous, the well's water is said to also mend souls. Every sip from that sacred spring is a reminder that God cared for a wounded young woman—and that God will certainly provide for us as well.

We all need God's touch. As Saint Augustine put it, "Our hearts are restless, O Lord, until they rest in you." In fact, we need God as desperately as our bodies need water. Often, of course, we forget our need. We fill our hours with work, meetings, entertainment, shopping, and endless trivial pursuits . . . and, in the midst of it all, we often have the nagging sensation that something is missing. We want peace deeper than the absence of strife, rest more than a good night's sleep, and love so tender that no mere mortal can provide it.

A Hebrew poet wrote three thousand years ago, "As the deer pants for the water, so my soul pants for you" (Psalm 42:1). And the Sufi poet Rumi described his aching for God as being like that of a reed plucked from the water:

> *Since I was cut from the reed bed,*
> *I have made this crying sound.*
> *Anyone apart from someone he loves*
> *understands what I say.*
> *Anyone pulled from a source*
> *longs to go back.*

C.S. Lewis (a modern Celtic Christian, born in Ireland) uses the image of water to describe humanity's relationship with God: "If you want to be wet you must get into the water. If you want joy, power, peace, eternal life, you must get close to, or even into, the thing that has them. . . . They are a great fountain of energy and beauty spurting up at the very center of reality. If you are close to it, the spray will wet you: if you are not, you will remain dry."

The ancient Celts felt a sense of longing—almost of homesickness—for the spiritual realm, and they often expressed that yearning in terms of thirst. They regarded wells, lakes, and rivers as "thin places," gateways to other realms where they experienced magical healing. These were so sacred to the early Celts that they offered sacrifices of jewelry, armor, weaponry, and other such precious items to the deities through the springs. These sacrifices were of such value that when the Roman Empires invaded the Celtic lands, one of the Romans' first actions was to auction off to the highest bidder the local springs with the treasures they contained.

When the Celts were introduced to Christ, they discovered that the Bible gave them further reasons to associate spiritual blessings with flowing waters. In Genesis, Abraham's rejected servant Hagar wanders forlorn in the desert until God provides a spring to save her—and then she affirms, "You are the God who sees me" (Genesis 16:13). The psalmist described God's generosity by declaring, "He turned the desert into pools of water and the parched ground into flowing springs" (107:35). In the Gospel of John, when Jesus meets a Samaritan woman by Jacob's well, he asks her to draw water and then promises, "Whoever drinks the water I give will never thirst. Indeed, the water I give will become a spring of water welling up to eternal life" (John 4:4). In the next chapter of the same Gospel, Jesus heals a man who is paralyzed at "the pool of Bethesda," which was noted for its miraculous powers. And again, at the Feast of Tabernacles in Jerusalem, Jesus proclaims, "Whoever believes in me, as the Scripture has said, will have streams of living water flowing from within" (John 7:37). In Jesus' poetic language, the Holy Spirit is a well springing forth within us, and the Spirit gives us what we each need, the Divine Lover inhabiting our flesh and bone. Just as water is contained within each human cell—so that in large part we *are* water—so God promises to fill our lives with the Spirit. Down through the centuries, people have sought the living water Jesus described so long ago to the woman at the well.

Today, Christianity is a booming business—but some seekers in the twenty-first century find that megachurches and television ministries fail to quench their thirst. While many modern churches have adopted the technology and entertainment techniques of secular marketing in order to be culturally relevant, they nevertheless sometimes seem like ornate cups that are dry and empty inside. Unsatisfied with today's Christian culture, inwardly parched, some spiritual seekers have turned instead to older traditions for spiritual direction. Many of us who have encountered the writings of the ancient Celts find their faith still speaks with surprising clarity.

My own faith journey has twisted and turned. After I made a decision to become a follower of Jesus, I meandered through several Christian sects, attended a theological seminary, and served as pastor of three churches. During that time, I also worked in education and writing, and I became a husband and then a father, walking with two children from birth into adulthood. From the beginning of my spiritual odyssey, the Celtic saints intrigued me, partly because of their timeless answers to questions that were surprisingly modern, and partly because of my personal family heritage.

For years, I learned about Celtic spirituality through books and conversations, and then, in May of 2009, my wife and I spent three weeks on pilgrimage in England, Scotland, and Wales, including time at the pilgrim city of St. David's and the holy island of Iona. We drank from sacred wells, wandered through stone circles, and walked a labyrinth beside the ocean. The experiences we shared on that pilgrimage convinced us even more that the old Celtic ways connect powerfully with our modern-day spiritual yearnings.

The Deepest Waters

The Ancient Celts

"Proud," "boastful," and "high spirited" are words the ancient Greeks used to describe the people they called Keltoi, who came out of Eastern Europe around 500 BCE. No one is sure what the word "Celt" (or its derivative "Gaul") actually meant; it may signify "high" or "elevated," a reflection of their healthy self-esteem. The ancient Celts rushed into battles naked save for the torcs around their necks, overrunning what is today France, Spain, Switzerland, the United Kingdom, and parts of Germany.

Despite their penchant for warfare, the Celts formed orderly and humane societies. Communities were organized in *raths*, clusters of round wooden houses encircled by earthen embankments. They were farmers as well as warriors, their greatest treasures their cattle—essential sources of meat, milk, and cheese—and they grew barley, millet, oats, rye, and wheat. They excelled in the arts, hammering and engraving ornamental masterpieces such as the Gundestrup Cauldron and the Tara Brooch. They loved word-play and earth-lore.

Celtic women enjoyed rights unimagined by their Greek and Roman counterparts; they could marry or divorce as they chose, shared equal say with men, and owned their own property. A woman gifted with leadership qualities could ascend to be chief, and some Gaelic women chose to fight in battle. The warrior queen Boudicca gave much grief to the Romans.

The Celts practiced an elemental religion: they revered the spirits of lakes, rivers, wells, hills, mountains, and caves—the "thin places" where mortals could communicate with the denizens of Tir na n-Og, the spirit world. Female deities played important roles in the Celtic worldview; Ireland is named after the goddess Eriu, and the river Danube after the goddess Danu. On dire occasions, the Celts made sacrifices: pigs, cattle and, in worst-case scenarios, their fellow humans.

The druids (a word that translates "oak-wise") were the Celtic intelligentsia. Their teachings reflected the strength of trees. Female and male druids studied for decades, learning what we now call "natural science": medicine, philosophy, history, poetry, law, and several different languages. They served as judges, historians, and priests. Druids allegedly had powers of supernatural knowledge, and the stories of King Arthur's adviser Merlin show the value chieftains placed on these seers.

New Springs
The Arrival of Christianity in the Celtic World

When Jesus walked in Palestine, his people were chafing under Roman rule, and at the same time, the Roman legions were invading the Celtic tribes throughout Europe and Britain. By the time Christianity spread to the Celts, Rome rather than the Celts' own kings and queens ruled much of what had once been Celtic lands.

Saint Paul wrote one of his epistles to a group of Celts—the Galatians—in the year 55 CE. Centuries before, Celts had invaded the Greek world, advancing as far south as Delphi. Eventually, they settled in present-day Turkey where they were known as the Galatians (from "Gaels," another word for Celts), and this was the community to which Paul wrote his epistle. In it, he emphasizes liberty ("It is for freedom that Christ has set us free," 5:1) and equality ("There is neither Jew nor Greek, slave nor free, male nor female, for you are all one in Christ Jesus," 3:28). No doubt these themes resonated with the freedom-loving Celts.

The Christian faith probably arrived in Britain in the first century. Much later, legend would fill in the details: Joseph of Arimathea, accompanied by Mary Magdalene, Martha, and her brother Lazarus, settled in England's Glastonbury, bringing the Holy Grail with them. They built a church there, and today, visitors to this small town in Somerset can still touch the Holy Thorn Tree and drink from the Chalice Well. Though the details are

legendary in nature, Christianity did take root at Glastonbury in ancient times, and by the end of the fourth century, many Celts had converted to the new faith.

Early in the fifth century, Irish slavers kidnapped an
adolescent named Maewyn Succat, stealing him from
his home in what is modern-day Wales or Scotland. The
raiders threw him in the bottom of their hide-covered
boat and took him to their land across the Irish Sea. This
seemingly minor incident began a series of events that
changed world history. Maewyn had been raised a nomi-
nal Christian, but in bondage, his faith increased. Home-
sick, lonely, he prayed to God more than a hundred times
each day. Miraculously, he escaped from Eire (Ireland)
and returned to his family and home. More miraculously,
he heard God's call to return to Eire, and he obeyed,
bringing the story of Christ with him. Most miraculously,
by the time of his death, Maewyn—now known as Patrick—had persuaded most of the Irish to follow Jesus.
He did so simply by walking and talking, treating each
person he met with respect.

Patrick was a genius at cross-cultural communication;
he impressed the men and women of Eire with the essen-
tials of Christian faith, but at the same time, he affirmed
Irish culture. The result was a uniquely Celtic form of
Christianity that saw Christ not as a replacement for
earlier faiths but as a deeper fulfillment of them. Celtic
Christians kept ancient cultural features compatible with
the gospel without compromising their new beliefs. In

the New Testament, they read that God is at work where Christ is not yet acknowledged (see Acts 17:23, 26), and they believed God had been active among their ancestors before they received the gospel. As a result, theirs was a holistic world, without the dichotomy of Christian and non-Christian that the Roman church preached. Since Christ is "the true light that gives light to everyone" (John 1:9), the Celts looked for signs of God's illumination in all whom they encountered.

Patrick's disciples were eager to share the message of Christ, and in the following centuries, they spread their Celtic brand of faith throughout the British Isles and Europe. Historians credit these Celtic scholar-saints with preserving the ancient writings of the Western world from the destruction of the Dark Ages. Their pens were truly mightier than swords.

The Celtic followers of Jesus shared the basic forms of Christian faith common throughout the world, such as belief in the Trinity, the Apostles' Creed, and so on. Yet their spirituality was also distinctive; they theologized more creatively, artistically, and boldly than their contemporaries. True to their freedom-loving nature, they allowed considerable diversity in the Christian life, and they emphasized direct, mystical encounters with God. They were tribal people, deeply rooted in their lands, and their faith remained close to the soil, the mountains, the lakes, and sky. Like the knotwork patterns they loved, they believed spirituality was inseparably woven into life's every aspect.

Streams Converge
The Celts and Their Neighbors

Strangely enough, Celtic Christianity owes almost as much to an Egyptian hermit as it does to Saint Patrick.

Anthony of Egypt lived in the parched desert sands, shunning human companionship. He overcame ordeals that modern reality shows would never dare inflict on their contestants. Consequently, Anthony became what we would now think of as a celebrity. Pilgrims risked their lives traveling into the wilderness just for a word with him, and his biography became a bestseller. Other Christians followed Anthony into the desert. From their lonely hermitages, they battled demons and performed feats of spiritual athleticism.

These Desert Fathers and Mothers influenced many who heard of their spiritual exploits, and Egyptian ideas spread even to Ireland, Scotland, and Wales. The Welsh monk Rhigyfarch, in his *Life of St. David*, says that David, the patron saint of Wales, "imitated the monks of Egypt, and lived a life like theirs." Surrounded by Ireland's green lushness, Celtic Christians reminded themselves of the desert's spiritual value by using place names like Dysart (Westmeath), Desertmartin (Londonderry), Disert Oenghusa (Limerick), and Killadysert (Clare).

Historian William Dalrymple documents further historical evidence that the Egyptian Christians influenced the Celts. In a letter to Charlemagne, the early medieval educator Alcuin of York described Irish monks as "Pueri Egyptiaci" (children of the Egyptians), and an Irish monk agreed, writing that the Irish monks' achievements had been "transplanted out of Egypt." Archaeologists have dug up Egyptian pottery at King Arthur's legendary birthplace, Tintagel Castle in Cornwall; and Celtic Christians are known to have passed around tour books of the Egyptian desert monasteries. Ancient Celtic monks even carried small, richly decorated rugs, which they placed on the ground for prostrations and prayers, just as Muslims do today. (In fact, both Celts and Muslims adopted this practice from ancient Egyptian Christians.) Summing up all these historical connections, Dalrymple goes so far as to say, "Certainly if a monk from seventh-century Lindisfarne . . . were to come back today . . . he would find much more that was familiar in the practices and beliefs of a modern Muslim Sufi than he would with, say, a contemporary American Evangelical."

The flavor of Egypt infused Celtic Christianity, but other flavors were in the mix as well. The Celts' next-door neighbors, the Angles and Saxons, added their own taste to Celtic Christianity. As soon as Rome's legions had packed up and marched away from Britain, Germanic invaders pulled their longships onto England's shores, their swords whetted to battle the Celts. Their success can be gauged by the fact that we speak of "England" (Angle-land), and we call the days of the week Wednesday (in honor of the Anglo-Saxon God Woden), Thursday (after Thor), and Friday (for the fertility goddess Freya). Up north, the Picts prevented the invaders from coming over Hadrian's Wall, while in Wales and Cornwall, legendary Arthur is said to have fended off the Saxons. Due to these resistance movements, Scotland, Ireland, Cornwall, and Wales retained their Celtic languages and cultures. Meanwhile, the rest of Britain saw its way of life swept away by the tide of Anglo-Saxon conquests.

The Celts and these Germanic invaders faced each other at sword point more often than not, but there were also daily exchanges of culture, land, sex, and finally, religion. The Celts helped shape the faith of their new neighbors, and in exchange, the Saxons contributed their own cultural gifts. No one could ever argue that *Beowulf* is any way inferior to the poems of the Celtic bards!

Meanwhile, Celtic Christians also influenced other Europeans. Consider, for example, Saint Columbanus who was born in Leinster, then moved to Brittany, then on to Burgundy, where he established a monastery. Fueled by wanderlust and the desire to evangelize, Columbanus continued onward to three different locations in France, where he established more monasteries, and then further into Switzerland, where he did the same. Finally, this traveling Irishman decided in his old age to settle down at Bobbio in Italy, where he founded a monastery especially famous for its library. Hundreds of years later, that monastery put Celtic ideals (such as love for animals and nature) into the head of the most famous Christian saint—Francis of Assisi. The next time you see a Saint Francis statue offering water for the birds in a garden, picture Columbanus the Celt standing behind him!

Something ironic happened the week I wrote this first chapter. I began with that sip of holy well water from the little plastic bottle . . . and a few days later wound up in the local ER with dehydration.

Focused on bills to pay, lesson plans for an upcoming course, guests coming to stay, commuting by bicycle to meetings, and—I laugh now—writing a book titled *Water from an Ancient Well,* I forgot I live in a dry climate; I forgot my body's need for water. So . . . chest pains, nausea, and the fear I was having a heart attack sent me to the hospital. After a battery of tests, I was sent home with this reminder: "Don't get so busy you forget to drink."

Our spirits need a constant supply of living water as much as our bodies need H_2O. And some of the sweetest water is found in the Celts' ancient wells.

> *Come near me while I sing the ancient ways.*
> *—William Butler Yeats*

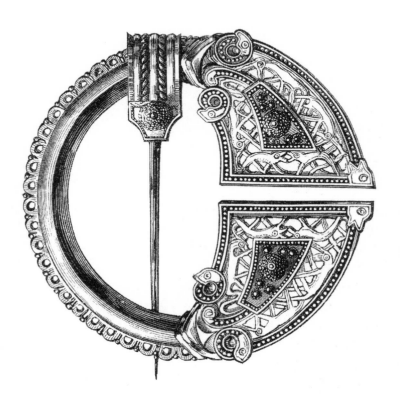

Workmanship like that found in the Tara Brooch and other Celtic jewelry reveals the ancient Celts' love of design and ornamentation.

2
The Spiritual Romance
In Love with Christ

As the deer pants for streams of water,
so my soul pants for you, O God.
My soul thirsts for God, for the living God.
—Psalm 42:1

"Everyone who drinks this water will be thirsty again,
but whoever drinks the water I give him will never thirst."
—Jesus (John 4:13–14)

Long ago—sometime in the late fifth century, the story goes—a teenage girl disagreed with her father, as young women often do. The girl was named Brigid, and she was beautiful through and through: her gold-brown hair gleamed like sunlight, and her laughter captivated hearts all around her. But for her father, Dubthach, an Irish chieftain, Brigid was just a headstrong frustration. She was of marriageable age, but she stubbornly refused all the husbands her father recommended.

Brigid's inner glow was fueled by her faith in Christ, a flame lit within her by that man from across the waves, Patrick. She had no interest in living the life of a wife and mother, and she had made up her mind to be wed only to the One she called Christ, a King greater in authority than her father.

But a neighboring nobleman heard of Brigid's beauty and came to Dubthach, seeking the young woman for his bride. He offered a generous price.

"Excellent!" said the chieftain. "You would be fine kin for our clan. I shall instruct Brigid to prepare herself for the wedding."

When he called on his daughter to tell her the news, Dubthach was braced for a fight, but to his surprise, she said, "Allow me to fix myself and then appear before this gentleman. If he is pleased, then I shall wed him."

The chieftain smiled to himself and went to tell the nobleman.

Alone in her chamber, Brigid put on her finest dress, combed her hair, and recalled words of Scripture she had memorized: *My lover is mine, and I am his . . . place me like a seal over your heart . . . for love is as strong as death, it burns like a blazing fire, like a mighty flame.*

She prayed, "Sweet Jesus, you know I want only to be yours. You have said, 'If your eye causes you to sin, pluck it out.' It would surely be sin for me to give myself without love to this man. So, my only true Lover and Friend, keep me for yourself only, and grant that I may—"

Brigid must surely have hesitated there, but then she squared her shoulders and set her chin. "Grant that I may pluck out my eye!" She raised a trembling hand to her right eye. She pushed, pulled, and yanked. . . .

Her eye popped out of its socket. It dangled from bloody strings onto her cheek.

Brigid bit back her pain and gathered her strength. Then she strode from her room into the great hall, where she stood before her suitor. "Sir, I have come as you wished. Do you find me pleasing?"

The suitor gasped, choked, then turned and hurried from the hall.

Brigid turned to the king. "Sorry, Father, he apparently did not find me pleasing. It must be my Christ's will I remain unmarried." She walked out of the room, not even waiting for her horrified father's reply.

Alone in her room, Brigid contemplated her grisly visage in a brass mirror. She smiled to herself. "No wonder he refused me."

After a moment, she whispered, "Jesus, you are my delight. Thank you for giving me the courage to be true to you." She paused. "My Sweet One, if you find me pleasing as I am now—for you look on the heart and not at the outward form—then I shall be content as well. But if you would allow me to be as I was before. . ."

Very carefully, she grasped the slimy surface of her severed eyeball between her thumb and forefinger, and placed it firmly back into its socket. Her face tingled. She blinked.

She could see through the eye again, she discovered. It was fastened in its place, perfectly restored. She daubed the blood from her cheek with a cloth, and poured out her gratitude in prayer.

There are many stories like this, telling of Brigid's strength of will, sense of humor, and passionate love for Christ. (You can read another story about Brigid in chapter 14.) It's impossible to totally separate the facts from the more fanciful strands that run through these stories. What all the many tales of Brigid's life consistently portray, though, is a woman ardently in love with the Son of God.

She was born somewhere around the year 454 and was named after the Celtic goddess of physicians, blacksmiths, and poets. Historical accounts of her life have been overlaid with legendary feats, but we do know she served as the Abbess of Kildare, an influential Irish monastery. She shares Patrick's status as the patron saint of Ireland, and at least one ancient account says she was a bishop.

The Greatest Goal
To Love God

Brigid and her spiritual kin thirsted for the living water that refreshes souls. They had fallen in love; they were enthralled with Christ. Brigid's only surviving written composition speaks of her desire to satisfy Christ's thirst, as he had so fully met hers.

> *I would like a great lake of ale, for the King of the Kings.*
> *I would like the angels of Heaven to be among us.*
> *I would like an abundance of peace.*
> *I would like full vessels of charity.*
> *I would like rich treasures of mercy.*
> *I would like cheerfulness to preside over all.*
> *I would like Jesus to be present.*
> *I would like the three Marys of illustrious renown*
> *to be with us.*
> *I would like the friends of Heaven*
> *to be gathered around us from all parts.*
> *I would like a great lake of beer for the King of Kings.*
> *I would like to be watching Heaven's family*
> *drinking it through all eternity.*

Brigid's earthy sentiments might upset the teetotaler conservatives of later times, but they well expressed the overflowing bounty of her love and joy.

The Celtic saints loved the good things of this Earth, but their passion for Christ inspired them to "keep first things first" in their lives. While they delighted in nature, they worshiped the Creator rather than creation (see Romans 1:25). As much as they enjoyed copying, illuminating, and reading sacred texts, they loved the God who inspired the Word more than they loved Scripture.

Water from an Ancient Well

They strove always to obey the scriptural injunction to "love the Lord your God with all your heart and with all your soul and with all your mind and with all your strength." Their thirst for Christ was unquenchable. The great Celtic saint Columbanus, as he moved throughout Europe, encouraged his friends: "Let us desire him like people who are ravenous . . . let us always drink of him with an overflowing love, let us always drink of him with a fullness of longing, and let the sweet savor of his loveliness ravish us."

The Celts sought to love God with all their being, and likewise, to love all of the Being that was God. As a result, they loved the Threefold God, the Divine Trinity. In theory, all Christians of the time were Trinitarian, yet the Celts took God's triune nature even more to heart. They filled their ordinary lives with patterns of three that reminded them of God's immanent presence in all life. Prayers like this one from nineteenth-century rural Scots reinforced their awareness of the Holy Trinity:

I am bending my knee
in the eye of the Father who created me,
in the eye of the Son who purchased me,
in the eye of the Spirit who cleansed me,
in friendship and affection.

Framed by their passion for the Trinity, the Celts focused their ardor specifically on Christ. In the

mid-eighth century, an Irish monk named Colcu ú
Duinechda of Clonmacnois wrote "The Broom of Devotion," a devotional poem filled with words of love for
Jesus, the "fountain ever-new," the spring that refreshes
our souls.

> *O holy Jesus,*
> *Gentle friend,*
> *Morning Star,*
> *Midday sun adorned,*
> *Brilliant flame of righteousness,*
> *life everlasting and eternity,*
> *Fountain ever-new, ever-living, ever-lasting. . . .*
> *Son of the merciful Father, without mother in heaven,*
> *Son of the true Virgin Mary, without father on earth,*
> *True and loving Brother.*

We hear a lot about Jesus today, but the Jesus
whose name is used so familiarly—as though we all
know exactly whom we mean—doesn't seem quite like
the Jesus the Celts knew. Today's Jesus doesn't always
shine with that same lovely light the Celts saw. And
as his followers, we don't always surrender ourselves
to him with the Celts' sense of helpless delight and
incredulous adoration.

As a result, the Christ we think we know may not
seem all that attractive to others. I know a young woman,
for example, who believes in a Divine Reality—but she

has trouble with Jesus, despite the fact that she attends a Christian church. To her, Jesus seems too exclusive, so limited in scope; she cannot connect him with the signs of God's presence she senses outside her church circles. What does this man—who (she believes) only concerns himself with the "faithful"—what does this long-ago, seemingly judgmental man have to do with the red and gold of sunset clouds, the silver splash of a waterfall, or the quiet voice that whispers in the wind?

If we could come to know Christ the way the ancient Celts did, we might have a very different perspective. For the ancient Celts, Christ was not merely the historical figure who walked on the Earth in the first century. He was that, and he was more: the divine Logos—the Cosmic Word that made the world (John 1) and the one "who fills everything in every way" (Ephesians 1:23). Yes, said the Celts, we can come to know him within the Bible and in the sacraments of the church. But he also comes to us in dreams and visions, in each human being we meet, and in the natural world. The blazing sun itself is a display of Christ's love, as are the sound of the wind and the ripple of water. The Celts' passion for Christ did not make them narrow people mincing their way cautiously through life lest they fall into sin. On the contrary, their faith inspired them to open their hearts wider, to embrace nature and society more generously, since they found Christ revealed everywhere in the everyday world.

A medieval Welsh composition called *The Food of*

the Soul describes a friar's vision of Christ, detailing the beauty of the Divine Lord in abundant detail. As the mystical experience ends, Christ says to the friar, "Arise and love me further as much as you can." The writer encourages his readers: "Then through true love and the whole desire of your heart, you should let your mind dwell on the great beauty of the Divine Child."

Our Heart's Desire
Falling in Love with God

Too often our concepts of God were handed to us within a tightly wrapped box. Whether we were raised as a fundamentalist, a Catholic, or a Unitarian—or raised with no religion at all—we inherit the God passed along to us, a God that is neatly defined. We interact with this concept in various ways, at various levels of comfort, but wonder, delight, and passion are often missing from those interactions. Ultimately, the world around us may seem far more present and real than even our most devoutly held religious beliefs.

We use the word "love" for many things. We fall in love. We love our family and friends. We love our home. We love our nation. We love our favorite sports teams. We love our cars and our computers. We love ice cream. Many of us would include God in there somewhere, but the material abundance and relational complexity of modern life overshadows whatever it is we feel toward

God. The Divine One is not *the* love of our life.

Some people would deny that, of course. Many "committed Christians" truly believe they have placed Christ at the center of their lives. They're unaware that they may have in fact buried God beneath other things. Spiritual writer Jack Deere laments, "Christians demonstrate a consistent tendency to put almost any good thing ahead of loving God. Some of us make Bible study more important than loving God. Some of us pursue doctrinal purity more than we pursue . . . Jesus Christ."

Jesus tells us what is most important in life: "Love the Lord your God with all your heart and with all your soul and with all your mind and with all your strength" (Mark 12:30). Love God with everything you've got: emotionally, intellectually, physically.

Modern Christianity exerts a lot of intellectual energy, analyzing and examining the doctrinal foundations of the faith. We sometimes neglect, however, to involve our body and emotions. How can we kindle the *passion* the ancient Celts felt for God? Sure, we can make an intellectual commitment to God, and we can *act* like we love God. Both are essential to any long-term relationship. But how do we rouse our emotions, in the way the Celts did?

Any long-married person knows marriage can't be built on emotion alone—but a marriage that had only commitment with never any romance would be dry and joyless. Romance seems to just happen in our lives, with little effort on our part: I fell in love with my wife, and I continue to fall in love with her. We don't generate that kind of desire intellectually; it sweeps over us like a wave. When I first saw each of my children, I knew I was utterly given to them, not by conscious choice but by a simple overwhelming recognition of reality. In our relationship with God, though—an invisible, intangible God—how do we fall in love in such an overwhelming, inescapable way?

The Christian scriptures tell us that *we love God because God first loved us* (1 John 4:19). Love is woven into our very identities, before we were even born. We came into this world from God, and in God, we live and move and have our being (Acts 17:28). At the end of our lives, we return to God—and in the meantime, every beat of our hearts, every breath we take, every drop of water we swallow, and every photon that brings light to our world comes to us as an expression of God's love. Scripture reminds us, "In everything give thanks" (1 Thessalonians 5:16); this was the ancient Celts' practice, and as we imitate them, delighting in the many everyday blessings God sends us, our emotions will be stirred with gratitude and love.

Mahatma Gandhi wrote:

> We may not be God, but we are of God, even as a little drop of water is of the ocean. Imagine it torn away from the ocean and flung millions of miles away. It becomes helpless, torn from

its surroundings, and cannot feel the might and majesty of the ocean. But if some one could point out to it that it is the ocean, its faith would revive, it would dance with joy and the whole of the might and majesty of the ocean would be reflected in it.

The reciprocity of love-from-love can only go so far, though. You might get tired of hearing your significant other constantly say, "I love you because of what you do for me." You would probably prefer your partner to say, "I love you because of who you are." As the eleventh-century monk Bernard of Clairvaux wrote in his book, *Loving God*:

> Love springs from the soul; it is not a business contract. A mere contract—I'll do this, if you'll do that—will never give birth to love. Love is spontaneous. True love seeks no reward, and yet it has its reward: the beloved. If you love something on account of something else, what you really love is that something else, not the apparent object of your desire. . . . True love never demands anything in return.

But as human beings, we rely on God to initiate the spiritual romance. The ancient book called the Song of Songs, long interpreted as an allegory of the Divine-human love affair, starts with the beloved saying, "Draw me after you and let us run together." It is the Divine yearning within us that calls forth our love. What a relief! The object of our desire wants us even more than we want the desired one! It is God within us that allows us to fall in love with God.

In *Loving God*, Bernard of Clairvaux went on to write:

The motive for loving God is God himself. He is both the cause of our love and the object of our love. He is the inspiration for our love, he creates our love, and he fulfills our love. Loving him comes naturally, because our love is prepared and rewarded by his for us. Some day we will love him perfectly. That is the hope that leads our love forward. . . . Here is a paradox: no one can seek God unless they have already found him. You, O God, write the rules to this strange game of hide-and-seek, allowing us to find you so that we can look for you—while we look for you, so that you can be more truly found.

Loving God is a lifelong pilgrimage, a labyrinth walk that in this mortal life never fully reaches the center point. Our affections wax and wane, rarely burning white-hot. We may have rare, intense experiences of Divine love, but ordinary life is generally not lived on the emotional mountaintops. This is only normal. As another great Celtic theologian, Julian of Norwich, wrote in the fourteenth century, "God allows us to feel a range of emotions—but they are all expressions of Divine love."

We shouldn't feel guilty or beat ourselves up if our passion for God rises and falls from day to day. As all long-married lovers know, that is the role of commitment: to carry us even when our emotions seem to flag, knowing that sooner or later our passion will surge again.

And we can take hope from these words from the Apostle Paul: "We all, with unveiled face beholding as in a mirror the glory of the Lord, are being transformed into the same image from glory to glory" (2 Corinthians 3:18). Even our dim, as-in-a-mirror glimpses of God are sufficient to change us gloriously. God takes our stumbling advances—and sweeps us off our feet in a Divine embrace.

Thanks be to You, Jesus Christ,
For the many gifts You have given me. . . .
I am giving You worship with my whole life. . . .
I am giving You love with my whole devotion,
I am on my knees with my whole desire.
I am giving You love with my whole heart,
I am giving You affection with all my senses.
I am giving You my existence with my whole mind.

Brigid's life is a good example of the ways in which passion for God spills out into the world. Under her leadership, Kildare became a center of both religion and learning. She also founded a school of art that included metal work and illumination.

3

Be Thou My Vision
GOD IN THE EVERYDAY

Happy are those who . . . delight in the law of the LORD. . . .
They are like trees planted by streams of water,
which yield their fruit in its season,
and their leaves do not wither.
In all that they do, they prosper.
—Psalm 1:1–3

Andy Rogers, an Irish musician, reminds his listeners of the connection between worship and ordinary life. He plays what he calls "ethno-Celt" music, blending folk, indigenous, and rock sounds. Over the years, Rogers has performed around the world, not only in spiritual assemblies but also in orphanages, bars, nightclubs—and even, on one occasion, a brothel in the epicenter of Asia's notorious sex-trade industry.

Musicians learn to know their audiences, carefully selecting tunes for each venue. Rogers has found that in places where many churchgoers might be scandalized, the audiences react most positively to an old hymn: "Be

Thou My Vision." Something in that ancient hymn's lyrics has a universal relevance. An anonymous songwriter composed it in Gaelic hundreds of years ago, back in the Dark Ages, but in 1912, Eleanor Hull rendered the song into its English form.

> *Be Thou my vision, O Lord of my heart;*
> *Naught be all else to me, save that Thou art.*
> *Thou my best thought, by day or by night,*
> *Waking or sleeping, Thy presence my light.*
>
> *Be Thou my wisdom, and Thou my true word;*
> *I ever with Thee and Thou with me, Lord;*
> *Thou my great Father, I Thy true son;*
> *Thou in me dwelling, and I with Thee one.*
>
> *Be Thou my battle shield, sword for the fight;*
> *Be Thou my Dignity, Thou my Delight;*
> *Thou my soul's shelter, Thou my high tower:*
> *Raise Thou me heavenward, O Power of my power.*
>
> *High King of Heaven, my victory won,*
> *May I reach Heaven's joys, O bright Heaven's Sun!*
> *Heart of my own heart, whatever befall,*
> *Still be my vision, O Ruler of all.*

These words remind us that God is as close as our own heartbeat, with us while we are "waking or sleeping."

God is there in our "best thoughts" and our truest words; the Divine Presence is always with us, a shelter for our souls while at the same time dwelling within in us, the "great Heart" of our own hearts, that which gives us both dignity and delight. As much in a nightclub and as in a church, God is present, for in the Divine Presence "we live and move and have our existence" (Acts 17:28). We can see God everywhere; God is our vision.

Anyone who has tried to keep plants alive understands their need for constant water. Farmers who live in dry regions know that without irrigation, their crops will not thrive. And in a similar way, we need the constant stream of God's Spirit. That does not, however, necessarily mean we must interrupt our daily routines for spiritual observances. We can take delight in God while going about our necessary tasks. Celtic spirituality teaches us to celebrate God in the everyday things of life. To quote psychologist Carl Jung, "Bidden or not bidden, God is present." Infinite Compassion is always there, irrigating our dry lives with its endless flood.

The Little Things
God in the Ordinary World

Some years ago, a publisher hired my wife and me to write a set of books titled *North American Indians Today*. Our work was based on interviews with First Nations people. I learned a great deal as we traveled around the country that year, and my understanding of my own faith was challenged and enriched. A medicine man told us, "We practice our spiritual beliefs all the time—whether walking, eating, or working, day or night—it isn't a 'Sunday religion' like the Christians have." Other Native folk reinforced this thought again and again.

The ancient Celtic Christians didn't have a "Sunday religion" either. Like traditional First Nations people, the Celts perceived the interconnectedness of the universe. According to psychologist James Hillman, indigenous societies often focus on actions that ensure "their feeling is in right relation with the world." So for the ancient Celts, God was not just in holy places and high ceremonies; Divine loving-kindness was equally present in farmyards and on fishing boats. They found it while they milked the cows and washed their faces. It spilled through every ordinary day.

The God described in the Bible is also an everyday God, involved in the sweat and grime of life just as much as with the sanctuary. God is everywhere; the psalmist wrote: "If I go up to the heavens, you are there; if I make my bed in the depths, you are there" (139:8). The Apostle Paul admonished, "Whatever you do, whether in word or deed, do it all in the name of the Lord Jesus, giving thanks to God the Father through him" (Colossians 3:17). Unfortunately, modern life does not encourage this holistic perception of life, and more modern versions of Christianity often separate "spiritual times" from ordinary life.

We think about God in church; we may whisper a prayer in quiet moments when we are alone; but how often do we sense our connection to God as we drive to work, as we do the laundry, as we talk to coworkers, or as we pay our bills?

The final words of Saint David, the patron Saint of Wales who is sometimes referred to as the Waterman (perhaps a reference to his practice of praying in the ocean), were *Gwnewch y pethau bychain mewn bywyd*: "Do the little things in life." Today, this is still a common Welsh saying. David was renowned for his holiness, but he did not focus on accomplishing enormous acts of piety. Instead, he knew that life's sacredness is found in the common stuff of ordinary days. "Do the little things" is actually a foundational lesson in spirituality, for in the little things, life's mundane details, we experience God's presence.

Ancient Christianity was rooted in this concept. Clement of Alexandria, a second-century theologian, wrote, "All our life is a celebration for us; we are convinced, in fact, that God is always everywhere. We sing while we work, we sing hymns while we sail, we pray while we carry out all life's other occupations." In the fourth century, John Chrysostom, the Archbishop of Constantinople, expressed similar sentiments: "You can set up an altar to God in your minds by means of prayer. And so it is fitting to pray at your trade, on a journey, standing at a counter, or sitting at your handicraft." These attitudes toward faith were part of the bedrock from which Celtic spirituality grew.

Water from an Ancient Well

The collection of writings known as the *Carmina Gadelica* reveals the everyday nature of the Celts' faith. At the end of the nineteenth century, Alexander Carmichael compiled these Gaelic prayers, songs, and sayings; the people of the Scottish Highlands had handed them down from person to person over long centuries. The daily repetition of prayers like this one reminded these Celtic Christians that God is never far away:

God with me lying down,
God with me rising up,
God with me in each ray of light,
And I have no ray of joy without Him,
Not one ray without Him.
Christ with me sleeping,
Christ with me waking,
Christ with me watching,
Every day and night,
Each day and night.
God with me protecting,
The Lord with me directing,
The Spirit with me strengthening,
For ever and for evermore,
Ever and evermore, Amen.

The poems in the *Carmina Gadelica* encompass all the rhythms of a day—waking, working, eating, and sleeping— and they also celebrate the lunar and solar seasons, as well as the year's holidays. Each day of the calendar was a new reminder of God's presence. Every ordinary task—starting a fire, planting seed, harvesting, milking, weaving, and caring for a baby—was yet another reminder of the Divine Presence beside and within them.

Smooring the fire—dampening the fire at night so it would not go out during the hours while the household slept—was one of the daily chores that called to mind God's presence in the lives of these long-ago Celts. In the damp and often chilly Highlands, the hearth was truly the life of the home, and if the fire died on a winter night, the household would wake to an ice-cold house. Some Scots boasted their fire had remained lit for generations. There was even a saying that, "If the fire dies out, the soul goes out of the people." Alexander Carmichael described the ritual that accompanied each night's smooring:

> The embers are evenly spread on the hearth—which is generally in the middle of the floor—and formed into a circle. This circle is then divided into three equal sections. . . . A peat is laid between each section. . . . The first peat is laid down in name of the God of Life, the second in name of the God of Peace, the third in name of the God of Grace. The circle is then covered over with ashes sufficient to subdue but not to extinguish the fire, in name of the Three of Light.

When the smooring process was complete, the woman (for women were the hearth-keepers) closed her eyes, stretched out her hand, and softly intoned a prayer such as this one:

> *The Sacred Three*
> *Our fortress be,*
> *Encircling we*
> *Who live within these walls.*
> *Come and be round*
> *Our hearth, our home.*
> *Protect this family*
> *And every sleeping thing*
> *Within this house*
> *From harm, from sin.*
> *Your care's our peace*
> *Through dark of night*
> *Till light's release.*

The rituals recorded in the *Carmina Gadelica* portray a way of life that affirmed God's reality in each of life's smallest moments. These Celts were never truly alone. God was their vision each moment of every day.

Spiritual Awareness
God as Your Vision

The ancient Celts' spiritual awareness sprang in part from their connections to the Christians of the Middle East—and religious practices there often came in turn from Jesus'

Jewish heritage. Jews have a long history of structuring their lives around blessings, creating a conscious framework that reminds them of God's everyday presence.

The Jewish *mezuzah* is a good example of this. The mezuzah (the Hebrew word for "doorpost") is a tiny scroll within a decorative case that is fastened to the doorframe of a home's entry. The scroll contains these words from the Torah: "Hear, O Israel: The Lord our God, the Lord is one. Love the Lord your God with all your heart and with all your soul and with all your strength. These commandments that I give you today are to be upon your hearts. . . . Write them on the doorframes of your houses and on your gates" (Deuteronomy 6:4–6, 9). Each time a Jew enters her home, she will touch the mezuzah and then kiss the fingertips that touched it. She may also say a prayer: "May God protect my going out and coming in, now and forever."

If we too were to practice this Jewish tradition, we might find that our daily homecomings (from work, from running errands, from wherever our lives take us) became sacred moments of connection with God. Christian theologian Leonard Sweet urges us to "mezuzah our universe." If we extend the concept of the mezuzah, Sweet says, we will find that "to mezuzah your universe is to live in a God environment."

Muslim believers also incorporate prayer into daily life by faithfully turning toward Mecca five times each day and kneeling in prayer. Nothing interferes with their practice of this routine; I've seen Muslims kneeling on their prayer rugs in busy airports, in the midst of a construction site, and on college campuses. Islam means "peace" or "submission to God," and we should all be challenged by Muslims' willingness to act out their peaceful submission to the Holy One in such a counter-cultural way. When Huston Smith, the Methodist author of *The World's Religions*, embraced the Muslim habit of praying five times daily, he found that God seemed much nearer throughout the day. Imagine if your own life was structured around prayer in such a daily, habit-ual way. How might your perceptions of life—and God— be changed?

We sometimes imagine that the great spiritual mystics had amazing, spontaneous experiences that came to them out of the blue. Sometimes they did, but almost always, those experiences were built on a daily prayer routine, a habit that sustained their relationship with God throughout all the various demands of their lives. "But things are dif-ferent now!" we tell ourselves. Our lives seem too chaotic to tame with even the simplest routines; amid the mad scramble of work and family, text messages and e-mail, daily commutes and late-night responsibilities, housework and meals, bills and phone calls, how can we find time for even the smallest moments of quiet prayer?

You don't need to kneel in public, though, to allow prayer to stream into each day's ordinary flow. Instead, you might get into the habit of waking up with a prayer, a simple "Good morning, God" when you first open your eyes. Or you might borrow from the ancient Celts and whisper this prayer as you get up:

The first word I say
In the morning when I arise
May it be Your Name.
May that Name be the armor I wear.
I shall put on the protection of the Christ today.

At the end of the day, you might say as you go to bed, "Good night, God. Thank you for today." Or again, if you wanted to imitate the Celtic Christians, you might use this prayer from the *Carmina Gadelica*:

I am placing my soul and my body
On Your sanctuary this night, O God,
On Your sanctuary, O Jesus Christ,
On Your sanctuary, O Spirit of perfect truth,
The Three who would defend my cause,
And not turn Their backs upon me.

O Creator, who is kind and just,
O Child, who overcame death,
O Holy Spirit of power,
Keep me this night from harm;
The Three who would justify me
Keep me this night and always.

Water from an Ancient Well

Monastic communities have traditionally used the sound of bells as calls to prayer, reminders to turn their thoughts toward God, but you can choose other triggers to serve the same function in your own life. Sitting at a red light, for instance, might be an occasion for prayer; a cup of coffee in your hand could be as well; even the sound of the telephone ringing (or the vibration of the cell phone in your pocket) could be the reminder that makes you silently say, "May my words praise you, oh Lord."

For a decade of my life, I taught in inner-city Los Angeles, and despite my best efforts, my classroom was at best, controlled chaos. In that hectic environment, I set my wristwatch to beep every hour as a brief reminder of God's presence. More than once, just as I was ready to go ballistic, thinking, *If Rafael shoots one more spit wad, the LAPD is going to have a homicide on their hands*, my wristwatch would beep: time for a tiny moment of prayer. *Thank you, Lord, for being with me.* Inevitably, after even that small restructuring of my awareness, I found my students more likable and the situation more manageable.

In Isaiah 49:16, God says, "I have engraved you on the palms of my hands." On a particularly demanding day, you might want to "engrave" God on your hands by writing a note to yourself, a reminder to pray. It may look messy, but even a single word or a simple design on your hand where you'll see it throughout the day can be the cue that directs your attention toward God. Some people have even chosen to make something like this permanent with a tattoo!

Be Thou My Vision

As we discussed earlier, the ancient Celts used each necessary daily chore as an occasion to pray, including getting washed in the morning. The *Carmina Gadelica* includes this prayer:

> *I am bathing my face*
> *In the mild rays of the sun,*
> *As Mary washed Christ*
> *In the rich milk of Egypt.*
>
> *Sweetness be in my mouth,*
> *Wisdom be in my speech,*
> *The love the fair Mary gave her Son*
> *May I see at the center of all life.*

Once again, the ancient Celts' practice was based on the Hebrew and Greek scriptures, where the act of washing is paired with consecration. Even doing the laundry was a holy act for the ancient Jews (Exodus 19:10, Numbers 8:21), as well as for the early Christians (Revelations 22:14). The Christian sacrament of baptism is also a ritualized "washing," one that we can call to mind each time we take a shower or wash our hands. By consciously identifying even the most ordinary acts with Christ's redemptive power, we sanctify both ourselves and our lives.

An object placed where we will see it often every day can also remind us to pray. This could be a mezuzah—or it could be a cross. For more than a millennia, Irish followers of Christ have decorated the entrances to their homes with Saint Brigid's crosses, woven from wheat or river reeds and sanctified by prayer, to serve as protection and blessing. (See instructions for making a Brigid's cross in the Appendix.) These crosses are made fresh each year on St. Brigid's Day (February 1), an annual ritual that creates a daily reminder of the Divine Presence.

In today's world, many of us spend almost as much time in our cars as we spend in our houses. So how can we "mezuzah" our vehicles? A cross dangling from the rear-view mirror is one option. And as with Jewish mezuzahs, we may want to make a habit of touching this small reminder, using tactile sense as well as visual to draw our hearts to attention. If we drive alone, daily car rides can even become habitual times of prayer that allow our vehicles to be transformed into moving "prayer closets," sacred places where we are shut away from the rest of the world with God. And at the very least, we should be sure to bless these machines on which we rely! A church in Los Angeles has the custom that every time a member acquires a new car, the whole church prays over it. The minister announces a "car dedication" following the Sunday morning service, and then the congregation goes outside, lays hands on the auto, and prays over it. They pray for God to protect the car and its passengers on the road, to provide happy and meaningful journeys. Prayers like these are much like the ancient Celts' prayers for their fishing boats—a practical way to involve God in everyday life. The book *Earth Afire with God* offers this modern "Celtic prayer" for car travel:

> *O God, defend me as I drive.*
> *May my eyes be sharp,*
> *My hands and feet sure.*
> *Deliver me from all danger on the road.*
> *Let the passengers who ride with me be safe as well.*
> *And protect each person I pass, each hapless beast.*
> *Guard my car with your great shield.*
> *May its tires run smoothly and its engine not fail.*
> *Let each part function as it should.*
> *May no harm come to me and mine as I drive,*
> *And may I do no harm to any other living creature.*

Of course, cars cause much damage to our planet, so we want might consider "the Holy Sacrament of Bicycling." Pedal pushing might not technically be a sacrament in the same way that the Eucharist or baptism is, but bicycling is surely what medieval theologian Peter Lombard called "sacramental"—an action that communicates God's grace. Biking transforms our perspectives: we feel the wind on our faces and the sun on our heads; we can literally stop and smell the flowers; and we encounter friends and acquaintances along the way. Each ride reminds us of God's presence.

Whether we drive or pedal to work—or don't go to work at all—we all have to eat. Giving thanks before each meal is a fine way to "mezuzah" our days, to build "grace" into each day's structure. But why do we limit thanksgiving to meal times? Author G. K. Chesterton wrote:

> You say grace before meals. All right. But I say grace before the play and the opera, and grace before the concert and the pantomime, and grace before I open a book, and grace before sketching, painting, swimming, fencing, boxing, walking, playing, dancing; and grace before I dip the pen in the ink.

Reminders of God's nearness can be something we do or say, or they can be something we hear or see or touch—and they can also be something we smell. Burning incense is one of the most ancient religious practices, dating back to the earliest humans, and incense is described as being part of worship and purification in the Hebrew scriptures (Exodus 30:7–8, Numbers 16:46). Many religions—from Hinduism to tribal religions—have used sweet-smelling substances to convey the Sacred Presence. Both Eastern and Western forms of Christian worship use burning censors to symbolize prayers rising before God (see Revelations 8:4), while other religions often consider sweet-scented smoke to be both healing and purifying. According to Proverbs 27:9, "Perfume and incense bring joy to the heart," and the psalmist wrote, "May my prayer be set before you like incense" (141:2). As the ancient Celts practiced their faith, so too can our own faith be rooted in the physical world around us, for God made all our senses—including smell—as ways for us to be mindful of Divine reality. As we breathe in sweet incense, we might pray, "Sweet Lord, sweeten all my life"—and when we leave the quiet of our prayer time, we will carry on our clothing the scent of incense, like "the pleasing aroma of Christ" (2 Corinthians 2:15).

When we begin to perceive life flowing together in a continuous sacramental stream, even the passage of time can serve to remind us of our connection to God. Scripture tells us "There is a time for everything, and a season for every activity under heaven" (Ecclesiastes 3:1). Living in our technologically advanced age, however, we sometimes ignore the changing seasons. We create artificial environments for ourselves, and in winter, we simply turn up the heat, while in summer, we crank up the air conditioning. Riding a bike to work—or walking *somewhere* daily—gives us opportunities to appreciate the seasons anew, but even the view outside our windows, the changing patterns of sunlight and darkness, snow and rain, leaves and bare branches, can all remind us that larger forces are constantly at work in the world beyond our small realms. Quaker sage Parker Palmer, in his book *Let Your Life Speak*, reminds us of the message that seasonal change brings: "We are participants in a vast communion of being, and if we open ourselves to its guidance, we can learn anew how to live in this great and gracious community of truth."

Water from an Ancient Well

In every culture since the beginning of human history, people have connected the changing patterns of the Earth and stars to underlying spiritual realities. The ancient Celtic Christians honored the Earth's passage through the heavens by observing the solstices and the equinoxes. They benefitted from having two sets of sacred seasons: that of their pagan ancestors alongside the newer calendar of the liturgical church year (the latter was so new that it was still being worked out when Patrick came to Ireland). They did not see these two sets of seasons in conflict with each other but instead found that one easily echoed the other. Modern followers of the ancient paths can likewise benefit from observing both the Celtic and liturgical calendars.

Many of the saints' days have accompanying rituals that help us grasp their meaning: for example, walking around the house and praying on Michaelmas (September 29, the feast day of the Archangel Michael), or blessing animals on October 4, Saint Francis's Feast Day. Celebrating holy seasons and special days creates a wave-like rhythm where daily variety and annual continuity stream together in a life-giving flow.

The Internet and books can offer guidance if we are starting these practices. An almost-daily guide is *The Celtic Year: A Celebration of Celtic Christian Saints, Sites, and Festivals* by Shirley Toulson, a collection of inspiring stories that includes hand-drawn illustrations. Another practical guide is Mara Freeman's book, *Kindling the Celtic Spirit: Ancient Traditions to Illumine Your Life Throughout the Seasons* (note that this book focuses more on pagan special days than Christian). Another fine resource is *Celtic Daily Light: A Spiritual Journey Through the Year* by Ray Simpson, which varies between a topical and seasonal arrangement, presenting thoughtful selections to pray and ponder for each day of the year.

Clearly, we don't have to leave our jobs or families and join a monastery in order to be immersed in the sacred. Doing the little things—observing sacred days, saying brief prayers throughout the day, lighting a candle, inhaling incense, or touching a reminder with our fingertips—can create a canal system of life-giving spiritual water. Without it, our souls may become arid and barren.

God longs to irrigate the everyday soil of our lives. All we have to do is clear the channels through which Divine grace can flow.

Faithfulness in little things is a big thing.
—Saint John Chrysostom

The ancient Celts' artwork also reveals their outlook on life:
the entire world is intertwined. The spiritual world and the ordinary
daily world, the world of nature and the human world, all form a
single strand, like the knotwork of which the Celts were so fond.

4
The Crux of Life
THE MEANINGS OF THE CROSS

One of the soldiers pierced Jesus' side with a spear,
bringing a sudden flow of blood and water.
—John 19:34

I awake feeling already alert; that alone is an unusual experience for me, because I'm not a morning person. Most days, I need to be prodded out of bed by several annoying rounds of my alarm, but not today. Sunrise gleams through the windows of our room here in this Welsh bed and breakfast, and I am ready for the dawn. Something is calling me.

I ease out of bed, trying not to disturb my wife, and pull on a pair of jeans, then creep down the stairs and out the door. Outside, fog hangs over the hills, softening their colors and shapes. I walk toward the sound of the ocean, past hedges and cottages. Cows gaze at me, then disappear into the mist, and rooks call in the air above me, flying in and out of sight.

I head across a field, past an ancient standing stone that tells me this is sacred space. As I pick my way around cow pies, I am reminded that the sacred and profane often co-mingle here on Earth. The ruined walls of an ancient chapel rise out of the mist, and I sense that this is what called me from my bed. Inside the broken walls, I find a weathered stone slab in the corner, as high as my waist and broad as my shoulders, incised with a simple wheel-cross. In Wales, the most ancient crosses, like this one, are etched onto boundary stones or gravestones.

I kneel before the stone cross. The only sounds are the mooing of cows in the mist, mixed with the endless rise-and-fall of the ocean's waves. All is at peace, and yet I'm filled with tremendous anticipation. With both hands, I clasp the sides of the ancient stone.

Immediately, I'm flooded with something I can't quite describe. Waves of energy roll through my body, from head to foot, again and again.

Later, I'll ponder these moments in my journal. Biology and psychology would say that the combination of internal and external stimuli had fired the endorphins in my brain, causing me to feel overwhelmed with positive emotions. Meanwhile, my metaphysically inclined friends would be convinced I had experienced the mind-altering properties of Earth energy. Pentecostals might recognize my experience as something akin to what they call the "Baptism of the Holy Spirit." Sophisticated religious analysts would call this "the experience of the numinous."

But at the time, I don't analyze the experience. None of those labels for the experience come to my mind, only a phrase that seems to ripple through me as each wave of energy passes along my nerves: *The power of the cross.*

Ɖeaven's Brigɥc Sun
The Celtic Wheel-Cross

That phrase would have resonated with the ancient Christian Celts and their neighbors. They believed that the cross was a powerful symbol.

In the beginning was the Word, say the Christian scriptures, referring to Christ. But what is a word? The Greek *logos*, translated "word" in English Bibles, literally meant the embodiment of an idea, the expression of a thought. Before words, before written language, humans relied on symbols to express their ideas. The ancient Greek word *symbolon* meant a mark or a token, an outward sign. Author and educator Jakob Streit explains that "among the oldest records of spiritual history are symbolic signs. . . . In all ancient cultures they precede . . . word or letter ideas. . . . The word *symbolon* had the meaning for the ancient Greeks 'to join what is separated.'" In other words, symbols were visual metaphors, something that carried meaning from one thing to another, so that humans could better grasp that which often lay beyond the reach of their physical senses.

Symbols continue to have meaning today, even if they have sometimes lost some of their power. Say the word

"Celtic," for example, and what symbol leaps to mind? Most people think of a wheel-cross, like the one pictured as part of this book's cover design. This ancient symbol has found its way into pop culture, appearing on t-shirts, tattoos, caps, and bumper stickers. Celtic has become cool—and the wheel-cross is its symbol.

The original wheel-crosses of Ireland, Scotland, and Wales, known as High Crosses, are still powerful symbols, monumental stones standing two or three times the height of a person, covered with interlaced designs that include geometric shapes, floral patterns, animals, and humans. The ancient stonemasons often depicted in amazing detail stories from the Bible—Daniel in the lion's den, David with his harp, Christ's resurrection, the preaching of the Apostles, and many others.

Historians don't really know why the ancient Celts were partial to the wheel-cross design, so we are left to speculate. Some experts believe the Celtic cross was an adaptation of the Roman Emperor Constantine's Chi-Rho cross. When Constantine adopted Christianity early in the fourth century, he formed a cross by combining the Greek letters "X" (Chi) and "R" (Rho), the first two letters in the Greek spelling of "Christ." Roman soldiers throughout the empire bore this insignia on their shields, so the symbol may have inspired the Celts.

However, this explanation doesn't quite work, since people of the British Isles used a form of the wheel-cross symbol *before* the Roman invasion. It's more likely that the first wheel-crosses represented the literal "light of the world"—the sun. The sun-circle symbols found in pre-Christian rock art contain horizontal and perpendicular lines, signifying the solstices and equinoxes; the four points are these four solar divisions of the year, while the circle is the sun itself. These markings are smaller portrayals of the prehistoric standing-stone circles found throughout the British Isles, such as Stonehenge.

Does this connection between sun worship and Christ-worship negate the power of Celtic Christianity? Not at all. Like the sun, Christ brings brightness, joy, and warmth; he is the source of all spiritual life. For the Celts (as for some Native believers in the Americas), Christ was the fulfillment of their ancient sun worship. He was truly both the Sun and the Son.

Patrick of Ireland, who did more than anyone else to create the unique flavor of Celtic Christianity, recalls in his autobiography an occasion when Christ came to him through the rays of the physical sun: "I saw the sun rise in the sky and while I called out 'Helia, Helia' ('Sunlight, Sunlight') with all my strength, behold the sun's splendor fell on me and . . . Christ my Lord assisted me."

In the ancient Celtic hymn "Be Thou My Vision," Christ is referred to as "Heaven's bright sun," and this metaphor of Sun and Son is implicit in Scripture itself. "I am the light of the world," Christ said. "Whoever follows me will never walk in darkness, but will have the light of life" (John 8:12). The Hebrew prophets also connected the sun with the Divine Presence: "Then your light will break forth like the dawn, and your healing will quickly appear" (Isaiah 58:8).

The *Carmina Gadelica* includes a morning hymn to the sun, an ancient Gaelic poem "giving glory to the great God of life for the glory of the sun and for the goodness of its light to the children of men and to the animals of the world":

> *The eye of the great God,*
> *The eye of the God of glory,*
> *The eye of the King of hosts,*
> *The eye of the King of the living,*
> *Pouring upon us*
> *At each time and season,*
> *Pouring upon us*
> *Gently and generously.*
> *Glory to thee,*
> *Thou glorious sun.*
> *Glory to thee, thou sun,*
> *Face of the God of Life.*

Pairing the sun and the Son does not detract from Christ's glory; instead, it makes the Divine Splendor tangible. Without the sun's energy, all life on Earth would cease, so our sun is one of the best metaphors for Christ "in whom we live and move and have our being."

The Hero of the Rood
The Divine Victor

For most Christians today, the cross points not to the sun but to Christ's death. The wheel-cross, however, contains a range of symbolic meanings. Perhaps most important, it reminds us that Christ the Crucified One is still the light of the world. Like other aspects of this ancient faith, the Celtic cross calls us to broaden our spiritual sight so that we can receive a deeper level of Divine illumination.

Recall again Jakob Streit's observation that a symbol joins what is separated. This is truly what the cross does, for it symbolizes the place where God and humanity were joined together. It is literally the crux of human history, the spot where Earth and Heaven intersected in the physical world. The Apostle Paul wrote that at the cross "God was reconciling the world to himself in Christ" (2 Corinthian 5:19).

Furthermore, the wheel-cross illustrates the conjunction of all things in the cosmos. The vertical and horizontal lines represent the union of Heaven and Earth, and the wheel in the center indicates that all things—the sacred and the secular, the physical and the spiritual—are gathered together in Christ's atonement.

C. S. Lewis, the great Celtic theologian of modern times, reminds us in *Mere Christianity* of the significance of the cross: "We are told that Christ was killed for us, that His death has washed out our sins. . . . That is the formula. That is Christianity. That is what has to be believed." From there, however, Lewis takes our thoughts in another direction, reminding us not to become overly dogmatic. "Any theories we build up as to how Christ's death did all this are, in my view, quite secondary: mere plans or diagrams to be left alone if they do not help us, and, even if they do help us, not to be confused with the thing itself."

Despite Lewis's warning, many Christians tend to see one particular theory of Christ's death on the cross as being "true" to the exclusion of all others. When we do that, we are falling into the danger Lewis described, focusing on our theories, our mental "plans or diagrams"—concepts we can understand—rather than the reality that will ultimately be beyond our comprehension. In his blog *The Rebel God*, modern theological thinker Derek Flood writes something similar about our experience of the cross:

> We shouldn't try to squeeze it into a formula, to domesticate it, because in doing so—in explaining and categorizing—we automatically reduce it to much less than it is. We need to think of these things in analogies, we need to seek to understand and explain, this is good, but we need to also realize that these are always just two-dimensional pictures of something much bigger. We should never mistake our limited explanation of something for the reality itself.

Unfortunately, we tend to do exactly that. In the process, we often separate ourselves from other Christians who may believe differently.

The theory of the cross most Protestants hold today is that of "substitution." It goes like this: all humans are sinners who deserve punishment, but God the Father chose to punish his Son in humanity's place. Scripture cited to support this view is Isaiah 53: "He was punished for our transgressions." While common today, this theory of redemption has only been popular since Archbishop Anselm of Canterbury promoted it around the year 1100, more than a thousand years after the birth of Christianity.

The Celts and their ancient Christian neighbors understood Christ's work on the cross quite differently; their understanding was based on the perspective of the "Christus Victor" model of atonement. The Christus Victor premise was that Jesus' death was not a legal settlement with God (God had to punish *someone* for human sin, so Jesus substituted himself for humanity) but instead, a battle against the forces of darkness. On the cross, Christ stepped into the human arena where we all confront death and the other works of Satan. Like the bravest of knights, he fought with these terrifying enemies and was victorious; he forced them to release humanity from their grip. This theology is based on passages like Colossians 2:15: "And having disarmed the powers and authorities (evil spiritual powers), he made a public spectacle of them, triumphing over them by the cross," and 1 John 3:8: "The reason the Son of God appeared was to destroy the works of the devil."

The film *Lord of the Rings: The Two Towers* presents a powerful picture of this battle against evil. In the dark caverns of Moria, the wizard Gandalf (a Christ figure in Tolkien's epic) stands against a fiery demon called the Balrog. As they grapple with each other, they both fall into a chasm, hurtling down into the Earth's depths, clawing and slashing at one another as they descend. As the wizard and demon plummet into this dark and fiery underworld, Gandalf's companions flee to safety. They are grief-stricken over Gandalf's apparent death, but later in the story, he reappears, now dazzling white and possessing even greater powers than before. He has defeated the Balrog and emerged victorious. In the same way, early Christians imagined Christ dying, battling with Satan in the nether realms, and then rising as the victorious hero.

In a world where battle was common and warriors honored, this perspective must have been particularly appealing. The ancient Celts and their Saxon neighbors spent long evenings around the fire extolling the triumphs of their heroes. Christ's feats were as brave and thrilling as Beowulf's, the Saxon champion who wrestled with the demon Grendel, descended into the monster's subterranean lair, and then emerged victorious.

THE CRUX OF LIFE

Lesser known than *Beowulf*, yet equally poetic, is the Saxon "Dream of the Rood," in which a talking cross (the Rood) tells its story. The cross has been badly abused—felled, nailed, and blood-soaked—yet it is now "the victory beam," bejeweled and worshiped. Saxon scholar Robert Boenig writes, "Christ is no sacrificial victim in this poem; he is a hero with whom a Germanic warrior could readily identify."

> *Then the young hero ungirded himself,*
> *He who was God almighty,*
> *strong and stern.*
> *He ascended the wretched gallows,*
> *mighty in the strength of many,*
> *when he wanted to redeem mankind.*

Afterward, "He rested himself awhile, weary after the great war." Finally, "The Son, mighty and successful, was victorious in that quest when he came with many, a host of spirits into God's glorious kingdom." Saxon bards sung this tale of Christ's death on the cross as though it were a warrior's victory song.

Many of the ancient Christian Celts would have known this poem, for they were a literate people who loved words. They not only studied the Christian scriptures but also other Christian writings, and the monks of the ancient Iona monastery included *The Acts of Pilate* among the treasured documents of their library.

Water from an Ancient Well

In this book, Satan rushes to hell after Christ's death on the cross, "fleeing in fear" as Christ pursues him. When Christ reaches hell's gates, he demands, "Open thy gates that the King of Glory may come in." The demons refuse him entrance, but then "suddenly Hell did quake, and the gates of death and the locks were broken small, and the bars of iron broken, and fell to the ground, and all things were laid open." Christ then frees a jubilant crowd of captives. Afterward, "all the saints of God besought the Lord that he would leave the sign of victory—even of the holy cross—in hell, that the wicked ministers thereof might not prevail to keep back any that was accused, whom the Lord absolved. And it was so done, and *the Lord set his cross in the midst of hell*, which is the sign of victory; *and it shall remain there forever*" (italics mine).

For the ancient Celts and Saxons, the cross was a symbol of Christ's heroic and eternal victory over hell and death. They believed if they descended to the very depths of hell, they would find the cross waiting for them, offering them hope and salvation even there. The psalmist wrote, "If I make my bed in hell, behold, you are there" (139:8 KJV), and the Apostle Paul was "convinced that nothing can ever separate us from God's love. Neither death nor life, neither angels nor demons, neither our fears for today nor our worries about tomorrow—not even the powers of hell can separate us from God's love" (Romans 8:38 NLT).

Gazing at the Victory Beam
The Crux of Spiritual Life

In today's world, theology often seems no more relevant than the medieval question of how many angels could dance on a head of a pin. And yet this robust ancient theory of the cross can speak to us still.

We all struggle at times with the fear that we may be our own worst enemy. Even if we put on a bold face for the world, we often inwardly hear a chorus of voices expressing regret, shame, doubt, and loneliness. No matter how tired we are of this gloomy self-talk, it never seems to go away. If only we could swap out this pessimistic, defeated spirit for one that is victorious over life's fray!

This is a common feeling that most of us have had at one time or another. In spiritual terminology, the longing we're experiencing is to "die to ourselves." This total surrender of the selfish "I" means letting go of the ego that overwhelms us with its anxieties, allowing it to be replaced by our real selves, the true identity that lies at the heart of each of us.

It's an idea that's prevalent in other religions, as well as Christianity. In Buddhism, for example, a person's ego is the source of attachment, anger, and greed; spiritual growth requires the death of this false self. Hindus speak of *moksha*, the moment when we let go of our egos and become one with the Supreme Lord. Celtic pagans perceived initiation as the death of the old self, allowing a new self to be born; old patterns and attachments must fall away for the soul to move forward in its path. Modern-day pagans speak of putting themselves "in Brigid's hands" (referring to the Goddess Brigid, predecessor of Saint Brigid); in doing so, they offer themselves to the Divine will, ready to be molded, shaped, and beaten into a new and more perfect form. This process is possible only by means of surrender; otherwise, the tool breaks or becomes deformed and useless. The ancient Jews also recognized the need for an inward, spiritual death, symbolized by the practice of circumcision, cutting off one's old life and self (Deuteronomy 30:6).

The Gospel of Luke records that Jesus said, "Those who would come after me must deny themselves and take up their cross daily and follow me. For whoever wants to save their life will lose it, but whoever loses their life for me will save it. What good is it for someone to gain the whole world, and yet lose or forfeit their very self?" (9:23–25). In the book of First Timothy we read that to reign with Christ—to share his victory—we must also suffer with him (2:12).

This is not a message we like to hear. It seems to go against our natural urge for self-preservation. Besides, everywhere we turn, the voices of our era encourage our egos' gluttony. As an example, pay attention to the commercials you hear. You'll find that each is designed to speak directly to that greedy, needy, clinging part of yourself: "Grab all the gusto you can get!" "You deserve a break today!" "Because you're worth it!" "Just do it!" In the garden of Eden, the serpent promised our first parents, "You shall become like God"—and we accept that invitation each time we place ourselves and our pleasures at the center of our world.

Ironically, however, the ego's unfettered pursuit of pleasure ultimately becomes enslavement. Our cravings turn into addictions—and we miss out on the universe's deepest and truest joys. As C. S. Lewis remarked in *The Weight of Glory*, "We are half-hearted creatures, fooling about with drink and sex and ambition when infinite joy is offered us; we are like ignorant children who want to continue making mud pies in a slum because we cannot imagine what is meant by the offer of a vacation at the sea. We are far too easily pleased."

The only true freedom is found in abandoning our egos; we must allow ourselves to be killed on Christ's cross. The "self" that must be crucified alongside Christ is not the *real* you, however; it is not that which the ancient scholar Irenaeus referred to as the "human fully alive that is God's glory." As Quaker author Parker J. Palmer writes, "There is a great gulf between the way my ego wants to identify me, with its protective masks and self-serving fictions, and my true self."

If we want to follow Christ, we must "take up our cross daily," surrendering our false selves. We must make the same commitment to God that twentieth-century martyr Charles de Foucauld did: "I abandon myself into your hands; do with me what you will." When we do, we can finally let go of the exhausting, endless pursuit of *things*; the craving for a new car, a bigger house, and a fatter paycheck will no longer pull us like a leash.

The word "surrender" comes from the older word "render": to yield, to give up. It's not an easy thing to do, and our egos seldom give up easily. Psychologist George Breed, in his book *Embodying Spirit*, tells of the "rendering man" who once came to farms to claim animal remains; he would "whisk the carcass away and assist its transformation into further usefulness." Breed concludes: "To surrender means to allow oneself to be totally rendered. It is a painful process."

But the ancient Celtic Christians did not shrink from this challenge. They joyfully chose to join their Hero as he hung from the cross; they willingly allowed their egos to be nailed down and rendered. They whole-heartedly believed that the surrendered/rendered life was one of freedom and joy. This perspective is the one found in the Christian scriptures, where we read: "for if the son has set you free you are free indeed" (John 8:36); united with Christ in death you are "seated with him in the heavenly realms" (Ephesians 2:6); and we can say with the Apostle Paul, "I have been crucified with Christ and I no longer live, but Christ lives in me" (Galatians 2:20).

But we humans are shortsighted creatures. Even with the best of intentions, we're more likely to obsess over a threatened paycheck or even an outbreak of acne than we are to focus on the joyful triumph of Christ. We all too easily plummet from the noblest ideals to the most mundane thoughts and behaviors. With so many distractions around us, how do we manage the "daily" part of taking up our cross?

Here too we can find answers from the ancient Celts. Unlike other more dualistic approaches to Christianity, the Celts never divorced spirit from matter; they always united their supernatural lives with physical reality. That's why they kept tangible signs of the cross always nearby. A crucifix hanging from a cord around the neck, a hand gesture made in the shape of the cross, or the towering stone wheel-cross in the town square were not magic amulets but solid objects that reminded them of reality's true nature. They claimed the cross as part of their daily lives, an aspect of their most intimate identities, as this ancient prayer reveals:

Christ's cross over this face I wear, and over my ear.
Christ's cross over my eye.
Christ's cross over my nose.
Christ's cross to accompany me before.
Christ's cross to accompany me behind me.
Christ's cross to meet every difficulty
both on hollow and hill
Christ's cross eastwards facing me.
Christ's cross back toward the sunset.

*In the north, in the south, increasingly
may Christ's cross straightway be.
Christ's cross up to broad Heaven.
Christ's cross down to Earth.
Let no evil or hurt come to my body or my soul.
Christ's cross over me as I sit.
Christ's cross over me as I lie.
Christ's cross be all my strength
until we reach the King of Heaven.
From the top of my head to the end of my toenail,
O Christ, against every danger
I trust in the protection of the cross.
Till the day of my death,
when my flesh goes into the clay,
And I shall once more take
Christ's cross over this face.*

Many Christians make the Sign of the Cross by placing a hand on the forehead, drawing it down to the chest, then gesturing from shoulder to shoulder, drawing invisible victory beams over the heart. This is undoubtedly one of the most ancient Christian practices; Tertullian wrote in 211 CE that it was an old custom already in his day. He explained, "At every step and movement, at every going in and coming out, when we put on our clothes and shoes, when we bathe, when we sit at table, when we light the lamps, in all ordinary actions of daily life, we make the sign of the cross." Today, some

Protestant Christians are uncomfortable with this tradition, but the founder of Protestantism, Martin Luther, wrote that all Christians should make the Sign of the Cross when they awake, when they lie down, when they pray, and when they feel tempted. Crossing ourselves is a good way to integrate Christ's death and resurrection into everyday routine; it's a way to take our faith out from the mental space inside our thoughts and into the realm of physical movement.

If you think about the cross as an instrument of execution, it may seem an odd symbol to have become so associated with Christianity. Celtic Christianity helps us see a fuller, more positive meaning. Ultimately, the cross is a sign of freedom. Its "victory beams" still speak today, just as the Rood did to the ancient Saxons. It shouts out: "You are cut loose forever from your ego, pride, and insecurities. You are loved, you are forgiven, you are free." The cross makes visible God's promise that nothing will ever separate us from God's love.

Then the young warrior, God almighty,
mounted the cross in sight of many men.
—translated from the ancient Ruthwell Cross
in Dumfriesshire, Scotland

The Celtic cross combines the ancient pre-Christian
symbolism of the sun wheel, the sacred circle quartered
by the four directions, with another layer of meaning:
the cross on which Christ died, creating the intersection
between Heaven and Earth, God and humans.

5
Streams in the Desert
The Divine Presence in Solitude

See, I am doing a new thing
Now it springs up; do you not perceive it?
I am making a way in the desert
and streams in the wasteland.
—Isaiah 43:19

Aled crept through the thicket of pines. He dared not step on even a single telltale branch, lest he betray his presence to the figure that moved a dozen paces ahead, gliding wraith-like between the trees.

His quarry paused, looked over his shoulder, and Aled drew back behind a tree, hoping his green-dyed clothes would blend with the leaves. He waited, listening. . . .

"You've followed me all day. Leave me alone." The voice held no emotion.

Aled jumped and spun around to face the speaker.

He was just a few feet away, behind him—but how was that possible? Only moments before, the man had been a considerable distance ahead.

But then, this was no ordinary mortal. Myrddin of the Woods was a druid, counselor to a succession of kings. So many legends clung to his name that Aled could never sort tales from facts. He tried to stay calm as he took stock of the form before him.

Myrddin's face was as lined as the bark on an ancient oak, and his gray hair hung in tangles around it. His clothes looked like dead leaves sewn together, so that he blended seamlessly into the forest behind him. He smelled—not unpleasantly, Aled thought—like damp alder or moist lichen. His expression was as inscrutable as a stump's.

Aled sucked in a breath. "Lord Myrddin—" He bowed and then continued, "I am chief huntsman for King Rhydderch. I have traveled a week from Caer Legion to these Caledonian woods, on bequest of the King and of Queen Ganieda, your sister. They beg you—return to the court. You shall be elevated to the highest position, given whatever you desire. The King needs your counsel, as many troubles beset our land."

Aled paused, waiting for a response, but the figure before him remained motionless, as if his feet had taken root in the soil.

Aled shivered, despite the warmth of the midsummer day. He had heard whispered back in the King's hall that the druid had been birthed by a wood sprite or fathered by the devil. The man's silence seemed unnatural, but he cleared his throat and forced himself to continue. "Lady Guendoloeana weeps for you, sir. She is still fair—indeed, the loveliest woman in the City of Legions—and she waits for you, despite your long absence."

Myrddin's arm moved suddenly, thrusting his twisted staff at the younger man. "Leave." The word sounded as if it had been summoned up from the underworld itself.

Aled would have turned then and hastened back to Dyfed, but he was afraid to return without the druid, for he knew the unpleasant devices King Rhydderch could employ when he was disappointed by a servant. "I–I heard how you fled to these woods," Aled stuttered, "in the days of Peredur, after the slaughter at Caer Glyddi. Surely, sir, it was none of your fault."

"Leave." Myrddin made a cryptic motion with his free hand, a gesture of magical meaning that frightened Aled more than the threat of a blow from the sorcerer's staff.

He took a step back and sighed. "I don't presume to be able to capture you, so I have no choice but to return empty handed." He shook his head. "You know what Rhydderch will do to me."

"The King won't harm you," Myrddin muttered, his voice as hoarse as a raven's. "My sister, the Queen, has been playing harlot with Badur of Ceredigion, the King's enemy. When you return, they'll be at war. The King will forget to punish you."

Aled's jaw dropped. "How–how do you know that? Did you receive messengers from Dyfed?"

The old man laughed without any real mirth. "Messengers?" Myrddin gestured at the woods with his staff.

"I have scores of messengers and a legion of servants, here in my domain. The finches and rooks whisper news from afar, the wolf barks omens, the alders whisper through their leaves, and the winds blow secrets all day." He swept the staff in a wide arc. "Have you not heard from the priests that the All-Maker inhabits creation? Here, I am one with the Source and the End, in infinite motion and unceasing rest. I need no humans to instruct me about the world."

Aled momentarily forgot his mission as he stared at the wizard. "You are a seer—you know things beyond time and space. Were you then truly sired by the spirits?"

Myrddin brought down his staff on the forest floor with a muffled thud. "No! I am a man like you. But I have freed myself from the world of human affairs, the world of feasting and intrigue, of lusting and hating. Too much human society fogs the mind. Here I dwell in the Creator's vast chapel. I see the High King in all his works. I pass through thin places between visible and invisible realms. And you dare . . . to ask me to return with you?"

As Aled retraced his path back to the King's court, he pondered the sorcerer's words. Around him, the forest was silent except for the rustle of leaves and the call of birds. He found himself listening to these quiet sounds in a new way. In them, for the first time, he heard the voice of a Presence.

The Life of Merlin by Geoffrey of Monmouth, a twelfth-century Welsh scholar, inspired this account of a meeting in the woods with Merlin the Magician (Myrddin in the Welsh language), in the days before he was King Arthur's advisor. Merlin is one of the best-known Celtic mythic figures, the subject of innumerable tales for more than a thousand years. In *The Life of Merlin* he is a druid (literally, a "truth-knower") who bridges the wisdom traditions of Christian and pre-Christian Wales. Geoffrey's Merlin is a mystic of the old order, but he is also baptized, a prophetic bard who reveals the mysteries of Christian faith along with visions of humanity's future.

Geoffrey's account emphasizes Merlin's need for solitude. After an especially savage battle, Merlin leaves the royal court for a hermit's life in the woods of Caledonia (modern Scotland), and he remains there, despite repeated attempts to coax him back to civilization. Living as a hermit, Merlin attains the full strength of his mystical knowledge.

Doing so, Merlin affirms both pagan and Christian traditions. Practitioners of the old religion sought supernatural power and knowledge by escaping from human affairs and living in solidarity with the natural world, while Christian saints pursued union with God by living as hermits in remote places. In *The Life of Merlin*, Merlin's sister Ganieda affirms his choice: "Happy therefore are those who remain firm in a pious heart and serve God and renounce the world. To them Christ who reigns without end, the Creator of all things, shall grant to enjoy perpetual honor. In company with my brother I shall dwell in the woods and shall worship God with a joyful heart." That statement captures a key belief of the ancient Celts: spiritual strength is to be found in the solitude of the natural world.

God in the Wilderness
Seeking the Divine Presence

God is everywhere at all times, yet we often remain blind and unaware. The scriptures stress the importance of seeking God: "Those who seek me find me," promises Proverbs 8:17, and in the Gospel of Luke, Christ says, "Keep on seeking and you will find" (11:9 NLT). Contemplative author Brennan Manning says that God is like a child playing hide-and-seek, who laments, "I run and hide—but no one comes to seek me." If we want to see God, we must look for the Divine Presence.

But where should we look?

Spiritual masters from many religious traditions emphasize that the first step is to escape the world's busyness. Alone, in silence, a seeker can begin to hear the Voice. As Mahatma Gandhi put it, "The divine radio is always singing if we could only make ourselves ready to listen to it, but it is impossible to listen without silence."

Hebrew and Christian scriptures also reveal the importance of time alone with God in solitary places.

Lovers never share their most intimate moments with the public, and lovers of the Divine must make holy trysts. Moses ascended the Mountain of God alone, and remained there forty days, to receive the Torah. The prophet Elijah heard God's still small voice while he was hiding all alone in a cave (1 Kings 19). Isaiah promised that the streams of Divine Spirit will flow in the wilderness (35:6). Jesus began his ministry by fasting all alone for forty days in the desert. Later, he spent solitary nights in prayer for guidance. Saint Paul, like his Master, prepared for ministry by spending time alone in the desert (Galatians 1:16–17). John the Revelator was exiled on an island when he received his mystic visions.

For Christians in the Dark Ages, the greatest saint after these biblical heroes was Anthony of the Desert—an Egyptian believer who became the model hermit. Early in the fourth century, while still a young man, he inherited his parents' wealth, and shortly after that, he heard this Bible text at a church service: "If you would be perfect, go sell what you possess and give to the poor, and you will have treasures in heaven" (Matthew 19:21). Taking this literally, he donated his fortune to charity and resolved to follow a life of *ascesis* (spiritual discipline). He trained under other holy men, learning to fast, stay awake for all-night prayer vigils, and sleep on the hard ground.

Desiring still-more rigorous spiritual challenges, Anthony moved into an ancient Egyptian tomb. His experience there was more terrifying than all the *Mummy* movies played back-to-back! When Anthony was sealed inside the ancient stone walls (according to Athanasius's *Life of Saint Antony*), the devil came to him and

> with a multitude of demons he whipped him with such force that he lay upon the earth, speechless from the tortures. He contended that the pains were so severe as to lead one to say that the blows could not have been delivered by humans, since they caused such agony.

Anthony overcame the demons and then decided to move further into the desert. En route to his new hermitage, he beheld a chunk of gold in the sand, but he resisted the temptation to pick it up and went on his way to an abandoned fortress far from human habitation.

Somehow, though he lived so far from the world, stories of his effective prayer and miraculous deeds spread to other believers. Visitors made long and dangerous treks across the desert to see him. When they arrived, Anthony refused to open the door of his enclosure, but he did sometimes give spiritual advice through a window. Visitors reported that they heard him inside the walls, thrashing and yelling, battling the assaults of evil spirits.

In this age of air conditioning, cell phones, and big-screen television, we probably don't see the attraction of Saint Anthony's life. If he lived today, we would be all too likely to dismiss him as a crazy homeless man. But in the fourth century, Anthony's biography was the most-circulated religious book (besides the Bible), and it remained so for another three centuries. Anthony was a spiritual celebrity, and the power of his life drove thousands of pilgrims into the Egyptian desert to emulate their hero.

One reason for Anthony's popularity may have been the contrast between his spirituality and that of the "Christianized" Roman Empire. After Emperor Constantine's conversion, many in the empire adopted the name of Christianity, while remaining as immoral as they had been before, when they worshiped Venus and Mars. Against this backdrop of cruelty and corruption, Anthony and other ascetics stood out as serious believers, "seeking first the Kingdom of God" rather than earthly pleasures.

Anthony's story is filled with demonic encounters; it almost reads like episodes of *Buffy the Vampire Slayer*. Modern readers will probably question his sanity, but in the Dark Ages, people never doubted the reality of evil supernatural forces. Anthony of Egypt and other hermits like him were seen as performing an important service for humanity; they were the real-life "Ghostbusters" of their day, brave individuals who drew evil after them into the barren places and there fought and defeated the demons, delivering ordinary believers back in the towns from a host of temptations and ailments.

Demonic warfare may have been one of the more spectacular aspects of a hermit's life, but it was not the most important. Egyptian mystics were convinced that withdrawal from society was a prerequisite to spiritual growth. They knew that Christ the Word dwells in all people (John 1:4), "but the cares of this world, and the deceitfulness of riches, and the lusts of other things enter in, choke the word, and it becomes unfruitful" (Mark 4:19). By fleeing from the world's anxiety, lies, and cravings, the Desert Mothers and Fathers found intimacy with God. In the most arid landscape imaginable, they immersed themselves in the living waters of the Divine Presence.

The *Lives of the Desert Fathers*, written by eyewitnesses in the fourth century, documents these radical believers' extraordinary stories. According to these contemporary accounts, by drawing close to God in solitude, the Desert Fathers and Mothers gained amazing powers, as this story illustrates:

> Abba Lot went to see Abba Joseph and said: "Abba, as much as I am able I practice a small rule, a little fasting, some prayer and meditation, and remain quiet, and as much as possible I keep my thoughts clean. What else should I do?" Then the old man stood up and stretched out his hands toward heaven, and his fingers became like ten torches of flame. And he said: "If you wish, you can become all flame."

People traveled long distances from the cities, hoping that the desert saints could perform miraculous cures for their illnesses—and many visitors reported that they were indeed healed. There were also accounts of miraculous provision: bread, fruit, and water would inexplicably appear when a hermit prayed for sustenance. Likewise, city dwellers sought out hermits for words of counsel; the desert saints could sometimes, by the power of the Holy Spirit, see what was hidden, or in the future, or at great distances. Again, our more cynical age dismisses these stories of signs and wonders. The people who had these experiences firsthand also found them to be nearly unbelievable; they often stated, "You'll find this hard to believe, but we saw. . . ."

As the Irish, Scots, and Welsh became Christians, they too heard these stories, and their competitive temperaments drove them to the highest expressions of faith. They were warriors of the Spirit, not be outdone, determined to give their all for Christ, and their ancient pagan background made them ready to believe that spiritual strength grew in those who lived in the woods. The druids were called "oak wise" not only because they were mighty like the tall trees but also because they had learned wisdom from the trees, birds, and animals.

The Hebrew Psalms and Prophets invite God-followers to times of stillness, for "in silence and in hope shall be your strength" (Isaiah 30:15). Likewise the druids, when faced with vital decisions, withdrew into extended times of solitude and silence, trusting that in utter stillness they would find direction. According to accounts written during the Renaissance but based on still-earlier oral traditions, the druids taught a form of meditation called *dercad,* which enabled them to withdraw their minds completely from the surrounding world. Practicing dercad, they attained the condition called *sitchain,* a state of absolute calm where the individual dwelled in a great interior peace. Dercad was also described as "refreshing the soul" and "becoming one with the Cosmos." Early Irish churches permitted the continued practice of dercad among their believers.

But now, as Christ-followers, the Celts had new models to follow as well. The druids had always had mystical visions and performed extraordinary healings; Christ's newest emissaries believed they needed to surpass those visionaries of the old faith. And to do so, they needed the strength of solitude. The British Isles had no burning sands like Egypt did, of course, but they had their own kind of wilderness that was as remote and challenging.

Skellig Michael, for example, is a finger of rock that juts straight up out of the ocean west of Ireland (the Gaelic word *skellig* means "rock"). The ocean surrounding the rock is so rough that the 15 kilometers from the mainland to the island are sometimes impassible even with modern boats and equipment. The tiny island has no natural supply of fresh water and little farmable land. And yet here, at the top of this jagged promontory, at the edge of cliffs that drop straight down to the ocean, Irish monks built beehive-shaped stone huts called *clochans.* They hewed out cisterns for rainwater and laid stone steps over treacherous passes. On this barren thumb of rock, for more than six centuries, they strove to grow spiritually. Here, in what others would have seen as a barren world, they experienced the richness of God's companionship.

Celtic saints gained a reputation for their life as hermits. The twelfth-century *Life of Saint Illtud*, for instance, describes the life of a man born in Brittany in the late fifth century. According to the story, he traveled to Wales and joined Arthur's army, but his observation of a fatal hunting incident revealed to him the brevity of life, and he made up his mind to leave the world behind. He built a reed hut in South Glamorgan, where he bathed daily in cold river water and stayed awake many nights in prayer. There, he gained a reputation for holiness and spiritual wisdom that attracted disciples, including Wales' patron saint, David, who pressured Illtud to establish a monastery. Illtud complied, but he never lost his longing for the hermit life; at one point he left the monastic community for three years and retreated to a cave, where he lived alone, fasting and praying.

Like Illtud, many of the Celtic saints oscillated between life-in-community and life-as-hermits. Celtic faith has always had a strong activist element—believers wanted to transform society—and yet at the same time, they realized the limits of human strength. As a result, women and men seeking spiritual perfection adopted a wavelike rhythm for their lives, at times intensely engaged in teaching and acts of charity, while at other times withdrawing completely alone to desolate caves or islands. In solitude, their souls were filled, so they could empty themselves in seasons of service—and then retreat again for refreshment.

Of course, Celtic Christianity did not require that everyone become hermits. As we discussed in chapter 3, spirituality *was* everyday life for the Celts. And for most people in the Dark Ages, everyday life included extended periods of solitude in the natural world. Lacking television, iPods, cell phones, computers, and cars, our ancestors were accustomed to the quiet sounds of wind and water and birdsong—and they were comfortable keeping their own company. Tending the house and garden, caring for animals, dropping nets in the sea—whatever they did, they could meditate on the Divine Presence. The natural rhythms of ordinary life provided them with plenty of opportunities for quiet contemplation.

Thomas Merton, one of the great twentieth-century spiritual writers, wrote that the goal of the Desert Mothers and Fathers was "purity of heart—a clear unobstructed vision of the true state of affairs, an intuitive grasp of one's own inner reality as anchored, or rather lost, in God through Christ." Like the Egyptian saints, early Celtic Christians sought that same purity of heart, whether living alone on a windswept island or taking time from a day's routine to practice dercad. That "unobstructed vision of the true state of affairs" was why Myrddin chose to remain a hermit in his woods.

Ordinary Hermitages
Contemplatives in a Busy World

We could all benefit from this clarity of vision. Yet for most of us, retreating to a skellig or desert is impractical if not impossible.

Richard Foster, a modern-day author and Christian mystic, writes, "In contemporary society our Adversary majors in three things: noise, hurry and crowds." Foster goes on to quote psychiatrist C. G. Jung: "Hurry is not *of* the devil; it *is* the devil." Foster wrote these comments thirty years ago, before the inventions of cell phones, Twitter, and ever-more portable computers. Now people chat on their cell phones while driving, lunch breaks are used for business, and multitasking is taken for granted as a requirement of nearly every moment of every day. We are seldom truly alone, away from the reach of other human voices—so how can we achieve the solitude where we might hear God?

The first step is to simply believe that time alone is a valuable investment, that it's not wasting time in our already busy schedules. Richard Rohr, a Franciscan priest who runs the Center of Action and Contemplation in Albuquerque, New Mexico, knows that action and contemplation are inextricably linked. We cannot change the world without first retreating from the world. Rohr says:

After eight years at the center I'm convinced that I must primarily teach contemplation. . . . I've seen far too many activists who are not the answer. Their head answer is largely correct but the energy, the style and the soul are not. . . . They might have the answer, but they are not *themselves* the answer. In fact, they are often part of the problem.

A vital second step in genuine spiritual growth is to create a place in time and space where communication with God can happen. We must flee to the wilderness, even if our desert is a very small one. Rohr explains, "The desert is where we are voluntarily under-stimulated. No feedback. No new data. That's why [Christ] says to go into the closet. . . . I must be 'nothing' in order to be open to all of reality and new reality." Finding time when you can be alone and uninterrupted may mean getting yourself out of bed twenty minutes earlier each day—or disappearing from work during a break—or going off for a half-hour walk alone after supper.

These times need to become routine, in time but also in location. You may be blessed with an actual "meditation room," a quiet corner of your home where you find tranquility. Maybe you have a favorite bench in a local park. Some of us are fortunate enough to have woodlands or desert canyons nearby. In a worst-case scenario, you might have to take Jesus' words in the King James Bible literally: "When thou prayest, enter into thy closet, and when thou hast shut thy door, pray to thy Father which is in secret" (Matthew 6:6). Your bedroom closet may not be an ideal hermitage—but it can suffice!

The next step is simply this: "Be still." Even when our bodies are quiet, though, our minds often go on thinking as busily as ever. It takes practice and discipline to shut them down. Learn to go into "standby" mode. True prayer is not your own mind pattering on endlessly; don't try and force God. As Rohr says, "You can't push the river."

Some contemplatives find a short prayer phrase is a good tool for quieting their thoughts, like the Jesus Prayer, "Son of God have mercy," or the very ancient refrain, "Lord have mercy, Christ have mercy." Others focus on a single word, such as "Jesus," and then allow even that to drift away as they sink into utter stillness. When the mind is finally quiet, you can embrace an inner emptiness where God has room to speak.

Stilling yourself completely, you free yourself from your ego; in New Testament terms, you "die to self." In this quiet interior place, you are freed from judging others—and judging yourself. You are free from the voices that say, "I must do . . . ," "I ought to . . . ," and "I should." You are even free from "I am . . .". When you are no longer aware of any "I," then you are able to enter fully into the presence of God who resides within you; now it is no longer you who live but Christ who lives in you (Galatians 2:20).

As you descend into this solitude, make no demands. Simply "be still and know that I am God" (Psalm 46:10). If you demand that the All-Maker must guide you, or speak to you, or even reveal Godself, you limit the Divine Voice. "Guard your steps when you go to the house of God. Go near to listen rather than to offer the sacrifice of fools, who do not know that they do wrong" (Ecclesiastes 5:1).

Don't treat God as though the Divine were an imaginary friend you could control with your mind. Instead, remind yourself that prayer is time you spend with a *real* friend, someone you are sincerely hoping to understand better. What will that person say? You don't know ahead of time. That's the whole point of listening to that person; you wait to hear what she has to say, so you can know her more deeply.

It's the same with God. We can't second-guess what the Divine Voice will say. Maybe "Get up and call your daughter," or perhaps, "I want you to start writing a book." It could be "You've been acting a little silly lately," or simply "I love you." Sometimes God just sits beside you with a smile or floods your soul with contentment. Only God knows what God wants to communicate to a person who is utterly still and receptive.

Building these quiet moments into our daily and weekly routines is essential, but sometimes we need longer doses of solitude. Annual or biannual retreats can help us find the spiritual strength to carry us through the rest of our busy lives. I went on a retreat like that a few months ago, a memory that still stays with me.

I'm in a little casita, a room ten by ten feet, with large windows on two sides facing out into the desert wilderness of central Arizona. A storm blows in, turning the sky shades of purple and deep blue. Rain drums on the window, and I watch the lines of descending drops blown almost horizontally at the glass. Ocotillo cacti whip up and down, like mad dancers in the tempest.

I sit in the unlit room, silently, while the forces of nature howl and pound outside my shelter. The parched desert floor soaks up the rain almost as soon as it hits. My spirit feels the same, as though I too am soaking up the storm. I feel like I'm being washed, cleansed from doubt and frustration and anxious questions. I have no thoughts of yesterday or tomorrow, or even the next hour. I'm as pliant as the ocotillo, submissive as the dirt. Words come to mind from a psalm: "The God of glory thunders. . . . The LORD blesses his people with peace" (29:3, 11).

After two more days here, I'm astonished by the insights I've gained. I came without demand or expectation, but the Great One has had plenty to say. I leave blessed with a visionary picture of my life, and with confirmation from a venerable spiritual director. My banged-up spiritual compass points north again.

How could I ever hope to spend time any more profitably than that? Over the years, I've made a three- or four-day retreat, twice annually, part of my schedule. I find this yearly routine allows me to keep life in perspective, while I spend only a week's vacation time to do so. Campgrounds or cabins work okay for these times of hermitage, I've discovered, but monasteries and retreat houses are better yet. Benedictine and Fordite monks spend hours every day devoted to prayer, and I sense something special and powerful about ground that's been bathed in intercession over a long stretch of time. Sometimes when I arrive at monastic communities, I palpably feel weight lift off my shoulders, a tangible sensation of arriving on holy ground.

However, even on hallowed soil, don't expect that the entire retreat experience will necessarily be pleasant. Confronting ourselves in silence is not always easy. One woman told her pastor upon her return from a retreat he had urged her to take: "I nearly went mad the first two days—I really thought I might become crazy." For the first time in decades, she had taken time to be still and listen to her own heart—and in doing so, she allowed a legion of unexamined feelings the opportunity to catch up with her consciousness.

Remember what the Desert Fathers and Desert Mothers experienced when they went into the desert! Whatever you believe about demons and devils, the descent into stillness and solitude often means we must confront the forces of darkness in some way. Most typically, our emotions will initially respond to silence with anxiety and even depression. Like it or not, we all have demons we've tried to sweep under the carpet. Don't run away from them. Dealing with them (with God's help) is a necessary step toward wholeness and spiritual growth. Once you've confronted the darkness, you will emerge stronger, better able to walk in the light.

You don't need to prepare ahead of time for a retreat like this; you just need to make up your mind to go and commit to setting aside the time. Once you're there, retreat centers often offer spiritual guides—or you could go with no more than a Bible, a journal to write in, a pen, and clothes for hiking. Pray for guidance regarding what to take along. You never know; I once found a science fiction novel very meaningful during a retreat.

After a couple of days in silent retreat, deep peace sinks into your heart. Immersed in profound stillness, you become as settled as a stone, as free as the wind, as boundless as the sky. All is good. All is God.

Of course, some seasons of life—especially when we have young children—make both long and brief retreats difficult to schedule. During those periods, seek out tiny quiet spaces in your life and use them for drawing close to the Divine Presence as frequently and habitually as you can. It could be your daily commute to work . . . it might be your morning shower . . . it might be even be your bed in the moments before you sleep. Claim that space as your personal hermitage, your private wilderness. Make a habit of seeking God there.

Sometimes even an imaginary place can serve as the wilderness. Abba Philemon, one of the Desert Fathers who was the first to write down the words of the ancient "Jesus Prayer," told his followers, "With the help of your imagination, find the place of your heart and stay there with attention." As grownups, we may have forgotten how to make-believe, but it's a skill with spiritual benefits. In the busiest, nosiest moments, let your heart take you somewhere still and quiet, somewhere wild and lovely . . . and for just a moment, spend time there with the Presence.

It only takes a moment. Leave your busyness behind and enter your "desert" (wherever that may be). God is waiting to meet with you, ready to pour out streams of Living Water.

The tree that grows beside the water
is fresher and gives more fruit.
—Saint Teresa of Avila

Saint Anthony's spiritual warfare inspired medieval artists to create bizarre portrayals of his battles with demons. Anthony's experience reminds us that we are both spiritually strengthened by time alone—and at the same time still vulnerable to the forces of evil. Christ himself had a similar experience, when after his forty days alone in the desert, the devil paid him a visit.

6
Green Martyrs
Spiritual Fitness

I discipline my body like an athlete,
training it to do what it should.
Otherwise, I fear that after preaching to others
I myself might be disqualified.
—the Apostle Paul (I Corinthians 9:27 NLT)

Suppose that you decide to join a fitness club. Before signing a contract, you want to have a look around the place. The receptionist gives you a pass and says, "You'll love this health center—it's all designed to help you achieve the highest levels of wellness."

First, you look at the weight room. There are all sorts of machines for leg-lifts, abdominal crunches, arm stretches, and so on. But surprisingly, no one is working the machines. A half-dozen men and women, wearing sweats, are in the room, but they all look rather pudgy around the middle, and none of them are exerting themselves. Instead, they're sitting in recliners—yes, this health club has reclining chairs in the weight room—and they're reading glossy magazines with titles like *Physique*, *Iron*, and *Muscle and Fitness.*

You scratch your head and decide to check out the adjoining room, a large space illuminated by floor-to-ceiling windows on one side. You see row upon row of running machines and treadmills. They look new and shiny, obviously state-of-the art. Yet, to your astonishment, none of the machines are in use. In front of the large windows, a bunch of unhealthy-looking people are decked out in sneakers and spandex as they lean back in more recliners, reading magazines like *Running Times* and *Cool Running*. Others are watching images on big-screen monitors of people running marathons or jogging through forests and canyons. In one corner, a few people appear to be having a discussion group. As you drift nearer to them, you overhear them earnestly debating the merits of rowing over running as a way to burn calories. But there's no smell of sweat in the air—just perfume and cologne.

By now you're feeling a bit confused, but you see a sign pointing to the swimming pool, so you decide to investigate one more facility. You walk down a set of stairs and smell the chlorine before you see the sparkling water of an Olympic-size pool. As before, the facility is tip-top—but no one is in the pool. The deck chairs are lined up in rows, though, filled with overweight people in swimming trunks and bikinis. As elsewhere in the health club, these members are also intent on their sports literature and videos. A few are discussing different brands of swimwear, and two individuals seem to be in a passionate argument over whether the butterfly stroke or the crawl is a better way to swim.

Troubled and exasperated, you head back to the reception area. "What on earth is wrong with these people?" you ask the attendant. "No one is working out. No one is weightlifting or running or swimming. What kind of crazy place is this?"

"Oh," the woman sniffs, "you must be looking for one of those *old-fashioned* health clubs, where," she rolls her eyes, "they make people feel guilty if they don't get on the machines."

"But this is a gym," you sputter. "Don't people want to get fit? Doesn't anyone want to work up a sweat?"

The woman looks offended. "Please, I hate that expression. Perspiration is just . . . yucky. Our members all agree that they're happier not exerting themselves—life's hard enough without making our poor muscles do all those unpleasant exercises. It's better to enjoy physical fitness vicariously, reading magazines and watching movies—all of which are provided as part of our membership package, of course." Her sour expression smoothes itself away, and she smiles sweetly.

"But you can't mean— I mean, no one is actually getting fit. All the people look so—well, unhealthy."

Her smile disappears. "No one complains, sir. You won't find a healthier atmosphere anywhere else."

An Ancient Path
Spiritual Exercise

This scenario is obviously ridiculous—but if you think about it, contemporary Christianity is often a lot like a non-exercising health club. On the surface, there's plenty of opportunity for spiritual growth. After all, many people still go to church, and Christian media is pretty sophisticated these days, including books, magazines, videos, and music. But does all that necessarily translate into a deep spiritual transformation? Think of the "religious" people you know: Do they seem to be growing spiritually? Are they well-adjusted, loving folks who have an ever-deepening experience of God? Or are they obsessed with the externals of Christianity—the literature (even the Bible), the top-notch "spiritual" facility, the small groups, the worship bands, and the spiritual "atmosphere"?

The word "discipline" was once a popular one in spiritual circles, but we don't like it so much today. We connect discipline with naughty children, with spankings and scoldings. Spiritual discipline may call to mind the evil albino monk who practiced self-flagellation in *The Da Vinci Code*. Most modern-day Christians, especially many Protestants who wouldn't dream of even giving up something for Lent, would say that such practices are unnecessary, even unhealthy.

After all, back in the 1500s, Luther revolutionized Christianity when he insisted that God loves us because of our faith, not our works. He was right, of course: we don't need to earn Divine love by performing certain acts or by denying ourselves healthy pleasures. God *is* love; the Divine disposition is kindness ("grace" in theological language), so we don't need to do anything to "make" God love us. Love is simply God's nature.

However, *our experience* of Divine love is another matter. A thousand things get in the way of our ability to feel God's compassion. We walk through life blind to the grace that falls everywhere around us. The spiritual disciplines are simply ways that allow us to experience more of God's kindness. As Richard Foster puts it, "God has given us the disciplines of the spiritual life as a means of receiving His grace. The disciplines allow us to place ourselves before God so He can transform us." You might say the Living Water is always there in our lives—but we'll appreciate it more if we have been sweating spiritually. Just as our bodies need exercise in order to be strong and healthy, so do our spirits.

Jesus used the image of a yoke to speak of spiritual exercise. It's a common Asian metaphor too; many people who practice Hatha Yoga may not realize that the Sanskrit word *yoga* means "yoke" and refers to any form of spiritual discipline. Jesus assured his followers, "My yoke is easy and my burden is light"—but he never suggested that there was no yoke. He knew his followers would need to practice Jesus yoga.

Paul the Apostle, who did more than anyone to spread Christianity throughout the ancient world, was clear on the need for spiritual training: "Train yourself for godliness" (1 Timothy 4:7). The Greek word that's translated as "godliness" had to do with a "heart-response" to God, while the English word "train" is used for the Greek *gymnazō*, the word on which our *gymnasium* is based. A gymnasium is a place to gain fitness, a place that smells like sweat. So Paul calls believers to exert themselves for spiritual growth. Paul's point is clear: "Get out of the recliner and onto the spiritual treadmill. In other words, start carrying your cross!"

When Jesus told his followers, "If you want to follow me, you're going to have to take up your cross," he was speaking metaphorically; he didn't mean all his followers should lug around a literal cross on their shoulders, the way he eventually would have to do. Instead, he was saying that we cannot grow spiritually without learning to let go of our selfishness, our need to have our own way, to put ourselves at the center of the world. Saint Paul put this into practice by denying himself through service to others, as well as through prayer and fasting. These were the methods he used to train his heart to respond to God. Down through the centuries, many of Christ's followers have also practiced various "exercises" that strengthened their ability to love God and others.

Our modern Western world tends to lull us into passivity. We simply suck in entertainment by turning on the television, an iPod, or the computer, rather than creating entertainment for ourselves as earlier generations did. It's all too easy to plop down on the couch to watch television after a hard day at work (where most of us sat in an office chair all day), rather than head outdoors for a run. That's why a slew of recent surveys warn us that the incidence of heart attacks, high blood pressure, and diabetes is rising. In a similar way, modern Christianity rarely calls for spiritual exercise. Churches remind their members of the need to attend services, give financial offerings, and volunteer for committees—but these activities are more for the survival of institutions than for the health of individual souls.

The ancient Celts, however, engaged in robust spiritual exercises; they weren't afraid to sweat. The stories of Anthony of Egypt inspired them. Anthony's Gaelic sisters and brothers wanted to know God the way he did. They read his biography closely so they could model themselves after him. They paid attention when Anthony spoke of *ascesis,* a Greek word that literally translates "rigor" and denotes spiritual discipline. Furthermore—and this had great impact on Celtic spirituality—Anthony insisted that ascesis required physical practices. Our spiritual and physical natures are not separated or at odds with one another, but body and soul are at all points intertwined. What affects our physical well being involves our spiritual lives as well.

For thousands of years, other spiritual seekers have also understood the spiritual value of physical sweat. Archeological evidence reveals that, like the First Nations people of the Americas, ancient people in Iceland and Europe built "sweat lodges," places of intense heat; a form of sweat lodge existed in Ireland up through the eighteenth century. Traditionally, sweating has always been connected to spiritual cleanliness. It's a way to purify ourselves, to free ourselves from the demands of our bodies. Today, Native American sweats often start with the participants fasting for an entire day of contemplation in preparation—and they emerge from the sweat lodge with a renewed and deeper perception of their place in the spiritual world.

Celtic Christians also understood the connection between a sweaty body and a disciplined spirit; they knew the more they sweated, the more thirsty they became for the Divine. The Irish preacher Columbanus admonished his hearers, "Let us desire Christ . . . let us always drink of him with a overflowing love, let us always drink of him with a fullness of longing" (Sermon 13 in *Celtic Spirituality*). The ancient Celts experienced their whole life as exerting effort in order to receive blessing: sow and then you reap; work hard in the fields, and you will eat vegetables; fish hard, and you'll have salmon for supper; tend your sheep, and you can wear warm wool in the winter. Life was an unending pattern of hard work followed by satisfying reward. They were used to working up a sweat. Likewise, they invested energy into spiritual pursuits, in order to enjoy the ultimate pleasures of God's presence. "No discipline seems pleasant at the time, but painful," we read in Hebrews 12:11. "Later on, however, it produces a harvest of righteousness and peace for those who have been trained by it."

Since God lavishes such great affection on us, we obviously wish to reciprocate—yet our thoughts and emotions often stand in the way. "I do not understand my own actions. For I do not do what I want, but I do the very thing I hate" said the Apostle Paul, and countless believers have echoed his lament. Anthony and other ascetics offer a solution to the dilemma of our spiritual condition: we can better train our spiritual faculties by subjugating physical desires. This is why the Desert Fathers and Mothers lived in the desert, shunning material wealth, wearing simple garments, eating basic foods, and often fasting. By doing so, they found a joy in Divine love that few have equaled.

According to Scottish theologian and historian Ian Bradley, Celtic Christianity also stressed "asceticism and holiness, self-discipline and sacrifice." This feature of the ancient Celtic faith is often overlooked today. Many of us find "Celtic Christianity" attractive, but few modern-day disciples undertake the rigorous self-denial that characterized this ancient faith. We emphasize the tolerance and ecological awareness of the ancient Celts, but ancient documents focus as much on the ascetic nature of the old Gaelic faith. Almost every description of every Celtic saint highlights some form of ascetic practice.

"Green martyrdom" is a term that sums up Celtic asceticism. A seventh-century Irish document describes the green martyr: "by means of fasting and labor he frees himself from his evil desires, or suffers toil in penance and repentance." This statement is worth unpacking, as it gets at the heart of Celtic faith.

Martyrdom does not necessarily mean we die in some bloody dramatic way for the sake of our faith. Instead, we follow Christ' admonition to "take up our cross"; we make Paul's motto our own: "I have been crucified with Christ" (Galatians 2:20). This is a *living* crucifixion; we simultaneously slay the false-self while we birth our new Christ-self, so that "I no longer live, but Christ lives in me" (Galatians 2:20). That's why the Celts referred to this as green—or living—martyrdom. It involved an inward attitude—"repentance"; it required strenuous effort—"toil"; and it took the shape of specific practices—"fasting."

Martyrdom is not a particularly appealing concept in the modern world, but we need to think like an athlete: we won't grow strong if we never sweat; no gain without pain. The Celts' focus was always on the "gain" rather than the "pain." They knew that when we are freed from our selfish natures, we are freed to more deeply enjoy God's love.

Fasting was an essential component of green martyrdom, and the ancient Celtic monks could not conceive of a Christianity that did not involve fasting. Every Wednesday and Friday they abstained from any food, all day. In addition, they deliberately simplified their diet. Most monasteries allowed only water, breads, and vegetables—no meat, fish, or eggs. Unlike modern vegans, the monks did not choose this diet for its health benefits but for the spiritual benefits of self-denial. (As an interesting side note, the monks *did* allow themselves a regular portion of mead or beer; very few Celtic saints went so far as to abstain from beer! And some monasteries were more liberal regarding diet; monks at Iona, for example, enjoyed a luxurious fare of pork and fresh seafood.)

As humans, we all have the tendency to take otherwise healthy practices to unhealthy lengths; eating, exercise, work, going online, talking on the phone are all good things that can be done to excess—and so is asceticism. Lovers are especially known for their excessive actions, and as passionate lovers of the Divine, the ancient ascetics often went to extremes (to say the least). In Syria, Symeon the Stylite achieved fame because he lived for thirty-seven years on a small platform on top a pillar; other "pillar saints" later followed his model. Two of the greatest Celtic saints—David of Wales and Cuthbert of Lindisfarne—had a habit of spending nights praying while immersed in the cold ocean, reciting psalms and risking hypothermia. Another practice was the "cross vigil," in which monks prayed for long hours standing with the arms outstretched, making their bodies a literal response to Jesus' command to "take up my cross."

Such extremes verged on self-abuse and led Protestants to reject *all* asceticism. Today, unfortunately, most of us associate asceticism with its abuses rather than more moderate and healthy practices. More recently, however, some have looked again at the values of spiritual discipline. Dallas Willard, for example, a Christian professor and philosopher noted for his deep ponderings and his practice of spiritual life, writes "Jesus and his disciples were all clearly ascetic." Willard then defines asceticism as "simply a matter of adaptation of suitable means to obviously valuable ends." He goes on to affirm that believers must include "bodily behaviors" to grow closer to God, since "whatever is purely mental cannot transform the self." In other words, we need to sweat.

Nowadays, few of us will feel called to live on a pillar, freeze while praying in the ocean, or wear a hair shirt. But we do want to grow closer to God. How can the ancient practice of green martyrdom assist our spiritual growth in the modern world?

Spiritual Routines
Daily Sweat

Many of us tend to distrust the spiritual practices of our parents' generation. We're disillusioned with Christianity that has "the form of godliness" but none of its real power (2 Timothy 3:5). We're jaded and cynical about things like daily prayer times, and we're quick to say, "That's legalism. We should just pray whenever we want to." The Bible does in fact exhort us to "pray without ceasing" (1 Thessalonians 5:17), but a daily prayer routine has real benefits.

We are creatures of habit. It's not just a cliché: habits define our lives. You're in the habit of brushing your teeth, driving your car on one side of the road as opposed to the other, not picking your nose in public, and showing up at work day after day. You don't have to ponder whether to get dressed in the morning or which road to take when you drive to work. If you had to consciously think about all those things, if you had to make decisions each and every moment of your day, you'd soon be overwhelmed by life's complexities. Instead, you can get through much of your life on "autopilot," satisfying all the basic requirements necessary for daily life while leaving energy and mental space for other thoughts and actions.

Unfortunately, we often fail to structure our spiritual lives with similar useful habits. As a result, being "spiritual" seems to require far more energy and effort than it might otherwise. Our spirituality tends to limp along at an unsteady gait, in spurts and starts. Imagine if you sporadically remembered to eat dinner—or if you only found time to brush your teeth once or twice a month. The effects of neglecting these seemingly small actions would spill out into the rest of your life. Eventually, your physical health would suffer. Failing to create healthy spiritual habits has the same effect on your spirit's well-being.

Ancient Christian practice included set times and forms of prayer, called "common" or "daily" prayer, usually done morning and evening. This was not considered to be a restrictive form of legalism but simply a useful habit. Today, since most of us don't live in a community of monks, a daily devotional book can be useful when establishing a prayer habit; several such books are written from the viewpoint of ancient Celtic faith (look in the notes for this chapter at the back of the book to find some suggestions). Once it becomes routine, a practice of daily prayer can become a source of sustenance for our spiritual lives.

Beyond the habit of daily prayer, periods of voluntary self-denial are spiritually valuable. The Catholic practice of "giving something up for Lent" is in fact a basic lesson in "taking up your cross." It is rudimentary green martyrdom. When we gain control over physical cravings—whether for alcohol, cigarettes, video games, fast-food meals, new clothes, you name it—we often discover a substantial gain in spiritual control; we have more room in our thoughts and emotions for God, more energy for our spirits. Our attachments to the physical world put us in bondage, but when we can say "I don't need you" to these attachments, we achieve liberation. This doesn't mean that the physical world should be seen as evil, nor are our attachments sinful. Healthy self-denial says, "I

have every right to such-and-such, and I am not 'bad' if
I wish to keep it—but I have chosen to voluntarily deny
myself this thing, in order to gain the greater pleasure of
mastery over my selfish ego."

We often take for granted the material luxuries that
surround us, but if we can disengage ourselves from
them, our spirits are free to grow. Even in tough economic times, most of us in the West live better than half
the world's population does; few people in history have
so confused "wants" and "needs." Choosing to purchase
less than you could—a smaller home, a used compact car,
or thrift-store clothing—is not just a sensible budget practice. It also helps you train your ego; it reminds you that
the universe does not center on you.

Fasting—intentionally going without food—is an ancient
form of self-denial, one that even Jesus practiced in order
to increase his intimacy with the Creator. Few of us would
want to try to fast for forty days, as Jesus did, but most
healthy people can manage to go twenty-four hours each
week without any food (but still drinking water) with no
harmful physical effects. In fact, according to many health
experts, a weekly fast can help purge your body of toxins. Furthermore, the sensation of hunger can be a useful
spiritual tool, a little twinge that reminds you to recognize
that you are living in a God-filled world. As you go through
your day hungry, you may find you see the sacred in your
everyday routine more clearly.

The ancient Celts understood fasting not only as

refraining from all food, but also refraining from certain types of food. Following their example, you might choose to go without coffee—or beer—or beef, not because these things are "bad" but as a way to master your impulses.

You might also want to consider "fasting" from other activities besides eating. A television fast, for example, can be particularly healthy for our souls. Or you might want to fast from the Internet or talking on the phone. This is not to say that any of these activities are necessarily bad or harmful. But by denying ourselves what-is-good, we sharpen our focus on what-is-most-valuable.

To follow Jesus is to be a "disciple" (from Greek, a "learner"), and to learn God we must practice "discipleine"—the physical disciplines of regular prayer time, of self-denial, of fasting. As we fall in love with Christ, as the ancient Celts did, we will naturally seek to give him more space in our hearts and minds. We will say no to some of our wants so we can be free to say yes to God. And we will be willing to physically sweat so we will be spiritually strong.

> I wish . . . a conscience upright and spotless
> before holy Heaven.
> Making holy the body with good habits,
> treading it boldly down.
> —from "The Hermit," eighth-century Irish anonymous poem

The Celtic Christians sought to identify in practical ways with Christ's ultimate self-sacrifice on the cross. The practices of green martyrdom gave them a physical structure within which they could learn to identify emotionally and spiritually with Christ.

7
Every Bush Aflame
God Revealed in Nature

You care for the land and water it;
you enrich it abundantly.
The streams of God are filled with water.
. . . the hills are clothed with gladness.
The meadows are covered with flocks
and the valleys are mantled with grain;
they shout for joy and sing.
—Psalm 65:9–13

It's a perfect day for mountain biking: not too hot but not yet winter here in Northern Arizona. The red-brown trunks and grey-green needles of Ponderosa pines fly past me as I steer my bike along the trail. All I hear is the swish of knobby tires on the earth . . . the wind's rustle through the pine needles . . . occasionally a raven's call.

The path meanders back and forth along a dry creek bed, then climbs uphill through rock formations where I have to gear down, stand on the pedals, and balance the bike. After a few minutes, the path turns next into a deep but narrow single track, and I fly downhill through a meadow, then jump across the dry creek bed—and begin an ascent up a wooded hillside.

Finally, I descend into another meadow and reach my intended destination, my "prayer rock," the place I've named "Aslan's Throne." The volcanic rock is twice my height, pockmarked by time, and mottled with patches of lichen.

I lean the bicycle against a nearby pine, take off my helmet, and walk behind the rock, where a series of natural indentations serve as footholds. Using these, I can climb to the top, where a rounded dome forms a seat. My mind tells me that my prayer rock's features are all the natural results of volcanic eruption and the erosion of wind and water, but it's hard not to see a Divine hand behind the shaping of this rock; it's a perfect outdoor sanctuary. And perhaps the Divine plan is even *more* miraculous when it takes a million years to work its way to fruition.

Atop this monumental stone, I fold my legs, turn my hands upward on my knees, and close my eyes. I feel I am rooted to the Earth, as solidly placed as the stone. I begin to pray, bringing to mind my friends, loved ones, people in need of various help, and the woes of the world. Then my thoughts turn to sheer thankfulness—for the forest, the sun, this rock . . . and then, my meditation moves past words.

Presence embraces me. The stillness has become preternatural. I can no longer hear the ravens or the rustle of pines. I open my eyes and find the scene has shifted subtly: colors are brighter, lines crisper, and . . .

Somehow, I'm looking both from my eyes and simultaneously from beyond my point of view. "I" am no longer here. My body has merged with the Earth, the trees, and the sky. I am one with the forest and with God.

I'm not sure how long this reverie lasts, because time seems to have stopped. It's like being in a still photograph, only intensely tangible. I've entered into what seems like the very edge of God's view of the world, pulled outside space and time.

Eventually, I come back to normal consciousness. I hear the raven cawing; I feel my haunches cramping on the hard rock. I stand, stretch, and clamber back down the side of the rock. Yet the sense of astonishing peace, of unity with God and the world, remains.

Most people can relate to the feeling of being closer to God in nature. It is both instinctive and biblical, and it's also one of the strongest elements in Celtic spirituality. This primal love for the Earth and its maker also has implications for environmentalism: God is the fountain from which all creation flows; and if we damage our world we dishonor its source.

Many faith traditions see in nature a revelation of its Maker. A Hindu teacher said, "Like rain in the river going back to the ocean, every drop of water that wants to go back to its source is a religious seeker." Poet Elizabeth Browning wrote, "Earth is crammed with heaven and every bush aflame with God," and Hebrew and Christian scriptures affirm this perspective.

In Genesis, God chooses the rainbow as a sign of the covenant made "with every living creature." The Lord promises, "Whenever the rainbow appears in the clouds, I will see it and remember the everlasting covenant between God and all living creatures of every kind on the earth" (Genesis 9:16). A rainbow is a phenomenon of the Earth's most basic ecosystem—tiny droplets of water in the atmosphere, refracting solar rays—yet God uses it to communicate Divine love for all beings.

In Psalm 29, David likens a thunderstorm to God's voice: "The voice of the Lord is over the waters: the God of glory thunders. . . . The voice of the Lord twists the oaks and strips the forest bare." In the New Testament, the Apostle Paul testifies that "Since the creation of the world God's invisible qualities—his eternal power and divine nature—have been clearly seen, being understood from what has been made" (Romans 1:20).

Before they knew Christ, the Celts knew that nature was their portal to a great spiritual reality. Wells, mountain crags, caves, and lochs were "thin places" that allowed access to the realm of spirits. In these temples of nature, the Celts sought physical and spiritual healing, as well as revelation. The salmon, the eagle, and even the tiny hazelnut, all were allies in helping humanity access the mysterious magic that underlay physical matter.

The Celtic saints affirmed their ancestors' instincts. They were careful not to worship nature in and of itself (which was forbidden by biblical passages such as Romans 1:25), while remaining fully open to the revelation of God's glory in the natural world. One of the most ancient Celtic catechisms, attributed to Ninian who evangelized Scotland before Columba came, asks, "What is the fruit of study?" The answer is: "To perceive the eternal Word of God reflected in every plant and insect, every bird and animal, every man and woman."

References to Celtic art, poetry, and liturgy that celebrate nature are too many to name. The Welsh poem titled "The Loves of Taliesin" (and attributed to that greatest of Celtic bards) is just one example:

> Beautiful it is that God shall save me.
> Beautiful too the bright fish in the lake,
> Beautiful too the sun in the sky,
> The beauty of an eagle on the shore
> when the tide is full. . . .
> Beautiful the covenant of the Creator with Earth,
> The beauty in the wilderness of doe and fawn,
> The beauty of wild leeks and the berries of harvest,
> The beauty of the heather when it turns purple,

Beautiful the pastureland. . . .
The beauty of water shimmering,
The beauty of the world where the Trinity speaks,
But the loveliest of all is the Christ
Who lives in all beauty.

For the ancient Celts, the Divine beauty revealed in nature was inseparably entwined with the strands of Christian doctrine. Christ's death on the cross, for example, was not just for humankind; it was a cosmic event that touched the entire natural world.

In the suffering of Christ, all creation suffered. For the Celts, this conclusion was inescapable, considering the closeness of the Creator to creation. The twelfth-century *Book of Leinster* told an ancient tale of King Conchubar, who asks Bucrach, a druid, what is causing some unusual changes in creation and the eclipse of the sun and the moon at their full. The druid uses his gift of supernatural sight and replies, "The Son of God is now being crucified." Blathmac, an eighth-century poet, wrote that at the time of Christ's death, "A fierce stream of blood boiled until the bark of every tree was red; there was blood throughout the world on the top of every great wood. It would have been fitting for God's elements—the fair sun, the blue sky, the earth—to have changed their appearance, befitting their calamity." Along a similar vein, Julian of Norwich, the medieval mystic, wrote, "I saw a great unity between Christ and us; for when he was in pain, we were in pain, and all creatures able to suffer pain suffered with him."

For the most part, the ancient Celtic Christians expressed the connections they saw between God and nature in symbolic form, through their poetry and art. One great Celtic theologian, however, produced a profound and well-thought-out theology of creation that combined ancient druidic insights, scripture, and the work of numerous Christian theologians. His name was John Scotus Erigena, an Irishman who lived at the beginning of the ninth century. ("Scotus" was the common designation for anyone Gaelic, whether Scotch or Irish, and "Erigena" meant "born of Ireland.")

Viking raids around the year 800 forced Erigena and other Irish believers to flee their monasteries, seeking refuge on the European continent. Erigena settled in at Charlemagne's court, where he became the emperor's chief theologian-in-residence. There he developed his doctrine of creation, a form of panentheism (literally, "all-in-God").

Unlike pantheism, which says all reality *is* God, Erigena believed all reality, including nature, proceeds continually *from* God. Erigena claimed, "The whole of reality then is God, since God is source, sustainer, and end." Erigena went so far as to suggest that we could not even speak or think about God if God had not incarnated Godself into the medium of physical matter; God as pure spirit is unknowable and cannot be explained by any analogy. At the same time, Erigena guarded against idolatry (any form of worship given to material objects) by insisting that "God remains transcendently above all things." In other words, all creation is God, but there is more to God than creation. You can worship God and not worship God's creatures, but all God's works—every beast and insect, every leaf and twig, and every puddle and clod of dirt—are communications from the Divine. As Erigena's admirer Christopher Bamford explains, "All things—human nature, the universe, each one of us—are divine lights, luminous theophanies. The universe, the human soul, is a vast light-filled discourse, every word of which is uttered in and by The Word."

Erigena's theology was condemned by the Church and largely forgotten after his lifetime—but it had scriptural backing. The fourth Gospel begins by affirming, "*Through him* all things were made; without him nothing was made that has been made" (John 1:3). The Apostle Paul agrees that "*in him* we live and move and have our being" (Acts 17:28) and "All things were created by him and for him. He is before all things, and *in him all things* hold together" (Colossians 1:17–18; all italics are mine).

Later Christian thinkers echoed Erigena's belief that the material universe consists of God. Julian of Norwich stated, "God is everything that is good, and the goodness that everything has is God." Russian novelist Fydor Dostoevsky wrote, "Love all of God's creation, the whole of it and every grain of sand. Love every leaf, every ray of God's light! Love the animals, love the plants, and love everything. If you love everything, you will soon perceive the divine mystery in things. Once you perceive it, you will begin to comprehend it better every day. And you will come at last to love the whole world with an all-embracing love." The twentieth-century Catholic priest and theologian Teilhard de Chardin affirmed that "the heart of matter is at the heart of God," and founder of the Iona Community George MacLeod insisted, "Christ is vibrant in the material world, not just the spiritual world." In our own time, Episcopal priest Matthew Fox declares, "I see the universe as a Divine womb and we're all swimming around in this soup." Erigena would have understood all these thinkers as kindred spirits.

If nature is the revelation of God's very being, it should not only be celebrated but studied, for to know nature is to know God. Working from this assumption, the Celtic thinkers of Erigena's age achieved some extraordinary scientific insights, discoveries that would be forgotten and not redis-covered for another seven centuries. Erigena and another Irish monastic, Dungal of Bangor, for example, observed the nature of eclipses and suggested two modern notions—a spherical Earth and something very much like a heliocentric planetary system. Another Irish monk, Fergal, suggested there might be "another world and other men or suns or moons." These Celtic monks living in the Dark Ages were imagining something akin to a Star Trek universe—aliens and all—centuries before Copernicus! Their thoughts, how-ever, were mocked, and they were accused of denying the "plain truths" of the Church and scripture.

Water from an Ancient Well

The Celts' creation-based theology also led to one of history's first attempts at ecological restoration. As Martin and Nigel Palmer explain in *The Spiritual Traveler: England, Scotland and Wales*, "Britain, as part of the huge Roman Empire, was exploited . . . thoroughly. . . . By the end of the Roman period, c. AD 450, many parts of England had been farmed out and consisted of vast areas of scrublands." Meanwhile, the unconquered Celtic regions of Ireland, Scotland, and Wales remained ecologically more robust. The invading Saxons depended on raiding and warfare for their subsistence, in part because the land they had claimed was unable to sustain suitable levels of agriculture. Later, as Celtic Christians moved into areas of England formerly held by Rome, their activities included, "a new form of agriculture: replanting forests; cutting new waterways to irrigate parched land; creating ponds and lakes, and most importantly, building upon the old Celtic sacred vision of the land, of all nature, to revive the very land and spirit of Britain. . . . In this way the Celtic and Christian traditions restored the sacred to the landscape and refounded settled life in Britain."

Christianity today faces accusation that its doctrines have led to the exploitation of the natural world. The ancient Celtics, however, had a far different interpretation of the scriptures, one that led to the ecological restoration of Britain. They cared for the Earth with committed labor, believing it was the embodiment of God's very being.

Reunion
Earth and Worship

For most of this book, the modern applications of ancient Celtic theology have involved *doing*—going from theory to tangible practice. In this chapter, the action called for by these principles is more self-evident: get out in nature and care for the environment. What we may need, however, is to re-examine our *perceptions*, discovering ways to consciously reunite care for the Earth with Christian practice.

Many modern Christians have fallen prey to bifurcated thinking: they see ecology as having no ongoing role in Christian life. On the other hand, others say, "I don't need to go to church—I worship while I'm alone in the woods, by the ocean, or in the desert." In both cases, Christian practice and the natural world have been artificially separated.

For the ancient Celts, this split between their Christian selves and their nature-loving selves would have been impossible; the two aspects of their lives were like strands of a single rope. Christ the Divine Logos equally revealed God to humanity through the scriptures, in the wilderness, in the meeting of God's people, and out on the ocean. Restoring a parched field to arability was an act of worship, and the rituals of the church underscored the importance of the Earth. As Philip Newell, former Warden of Iona and Celtic spiritual writer, puts it, "In the ancient Celtic mission, from the fourth to seventh centuries, the pattern for worship was to gather around high-standing crosses in the context of earth, sea, and sky. The emphasis was that creation itself was the Sanctuary of God. And it included all things."

We have torn the sacred from the Earth with disastrous consequences. Science and religion engage in bitter debates, though both are ways to understand the Mystery that is God. Ecology and biblical theology are set in opposition, though ecology is service to God's very being. Many people see God and Jesus as obsolete and irrelevant—if not destructive—in a world beset by scarce resources, global warming, and ecological collapse. We need to rediscover how "to perceive the eternal Word of God reflected in every plant and insect, every bird and animal, every man and woman" (in the words of Ninian's Catechism). Faith in Jesus and trust in God could empower more good on behalf of our world than we can imagine.

There are countless ways to get involved in efforts to restore the environment. Petition your local government to fund more "green" measures, help rebuild a forest pathway, remove litter from a nearby stream, or put solar panels on your house. Recycle and reuse. Make conscious and informed choices when you buy your food and clothing. And do all these as conscious acts of worship. Remind yourself you are tending to God, the very flesh of your Maker. Jesus' statement, "whatever you do unto the least of these, you do unto me," can be applied to land and water as well as to the human members of his body.

Get to know God by reading the Bible and spending time in prayer—and by deepening your understanding of the natural world. Gaze at the stars, attend lectures at a local university or nature center, watch wildlife and cosmology shows; learn about the tiny organisms that live in your body, or about weather patterns in your part of the world, or about the Big Bang and origins of the universe. This too is worship. Science and faith are not enemies; instead, a love for science can nourish your soul and glorify the Creator. The plants in your yard, the microbes in your body, and the stars in the sky are all expressions of the Divine nature.

We live in a world where God reveals the miracle of grace in sky and leaf and stone. Even the tiny droplets of water in a rainbow color the world with their message of God's faithfulness.

She could now think of the Father of Spirits . . .
as the root of every delight in the world,
at the heart of the horse she rode,
in the wind that blew joy into her. . . .
No wonder that with this well of living water in her heart
she should be glad—merry even, and ready for anything.
—George MacDonald, from his novel Donal Grant

The Celts saw God revealed in every leaf and tree and flower, in moon and stars and sun.

8

FURRED AND FEATHERED NEIGHBORS
CREATURES OF GRACE

He makes springs . . . give water to all the beasts of the field;
the wild donkeys quench their thirst.
The birds of the air nest by the waters;
they sing among the branches. . . .
He makes grass grow for the cattle.
—Psalm 104:10–14

On a Sabbath day in Columba's seventy-seventh year, the old saint who had brought the Gospel to the land that today is called Scotland came with his companion Diormit to bless the barn at the Iona monastery. After he had said his blessing, he looked at the two heaps of winnowed corn that lay on the barn floor and said, "I am happy for my beloved monks, because even though I must leave you, you will have a enough corn to last you for the year."

When Diormit heard these words, he was grief stricken. "Father, why do you speak of leaving us?"

Columba replied, "This day in the Holy Scriptures is called the Sabbath, which means 'rest.' And this day is indeed a Sabbath for me, for it is the last day of my difficult life on Earth. On this Sabbath, I shall rest after all my hard work. I hear the Lord inviting me to come home, and in the middle of this night, I will depart, at His invitation."

Diormit began to weep bitterly when he heard these words. Columba tried to console him as best he could as they left the barn and made their way back to the monastery.

Halfway back to Columba's quarters, his legs grew weak, and he stopped to rest by the side of the path. As he sat there, a white packhorse came up to the old man and laid its head on his chest. The horse had for many years carried the milk-vessels from the cowshed to the monastery, and it knew and loved Columba. It sensed that this beloved human would soon leave it behind, and it sighed and shuddered in sorrow.

Diormit waved his hand at the horse. "Shoo! Leave the saint alone!"

But Columba shook his head at his companion. "No, let it grieve. This beast knows what will happen to me tonight. It understands me better even than you and my other brothers do."

The old man stroked the horse's head, and then he blessed it gently.

Columba's earliest biographer, Adamnan, tells this story about the end of Columba's life. It wouldn't be hard to fill this entire book with other stories of the Celtic saints and their furred or feathered companions. The ancient tales are filled with holy Doctor Doolittles.

No doubt some of these stories are embellished—it seems unlikely that Saint Kevin really tamed a Loch Ness monster—but nevertheless, they show us the real affinity that existed between these people and the animals around them. The Celtic saints understood that God uses the Earth's living creatures to carry Divine love to humans. These little brothers and sisters of ours often have a deeper, wordless wisdom we humans lack, one that points the way to the living streams where we all must drink.

Many of the ancient Celtic tales involve birds. In Adamnan's *Life of Columba*, for example, he inserts this curious heading before the thirty-fifth chapter: "The Saint's foreknowledge and prophecy concerning a matter of less moment, but so beautiful that it cannot, I think, be passed over in silence"—and he then relates a story.

While Columba was living on Iona, he said to one of the brothers, "Three days from now, in the morning, you must sit down and wait on the shore on the western side of this island. A crane, a stranger from the northern part of Ireland, has been driven by the wind, and it will fall on the beach beside you, weary and exhausted, sometime after the ninth hour of the day. Treat that bird tenderly.

Take it home with you, and then nurse it and feed it for three days and nights. When the crane is refreshed and no longer wants to stay with us, let it go, so it can fly back with renewed strength to the part of Ireland from which it originally came."

The brother obeyed, and on the third day, after the ninth hour, he watched for the arrival of the expected guest. As soon as the crane came and lit on the shore beside him, he picked it up gently and carried it home with him. There he fed it and made it comfortable.

When that monk came to the evening meal that night, before he had told Columba a word about what happened, the old man said to him, "God bless you, my child, for your kindness!"

And just as Columba had predicted, after three days, the bird was ready to fly on its way. While the monk watched, it flapped its wings and rose up high in the air. With steady strokes, it made its path homeward, across the sea to Ireland, as straight as it could fly.

A legend about Saint Kevin of Glendalough in County Wicklow, Ireland, tells another story about the Celtic saints' relationship with animals. According to the tale, Kevin was praying alone in his tiny hut overlooking the shores of the lake, with his hands resting palm upward on the windowsill in an expression of praise, when a blackbird flew down and put a twig in his hand. Fascinated, Kevin stood very still, watching as the bird flew back and forth with more twigs until she had built a nest. All the while, Kevin continued to stand without moving. Then the blackbird settled down on the nest and laid her eggs—and according to the legend, Saint Kevin loved animals so much he stood there, his hand still outstretched, until the eggs were hatched and the birds flew away.

Yet another saint-and-bird story (this one more a bit more believable) involves Francis of Assisi. Francis lived in Italy centuries after the golden age of Celtic Christianity, but he was one of the Celts' spiritual children, since the legacy of Columbanus (who founded a monastery in the area where Francis grew up) had deeply influenced him. According to his ancient biographer, Thomas of Celano, one day while Francis and some friars were traveling along the road, Francis looked up and saw a tree full of birds. Francis "left his companions in the road and ran eagerly toward the birds" and "humbly begged them to listen to the word of God." One of the friars recorded the sermon, which overflows with Francis's love for God and Creation:

> My brother birds, you should praise your Creator very much and always love him; he gave you feathers to clothe you, wings so that you can fly, and whatever else was necessary for you. God made you noble among his creatures, and he gave you a

home in the purity of the air; though you neither sow nor reap, he nevertheless protects and governs you without any solicitude on your part.

Thomas records that the birds remained perched in the tree's branches as Francis walked among them, touching and blessing them. Afterward, Francis "began to blame himself for negligence in not having preached to the birds before," so "from that day on, he solicitously admonished the birds, all animals and reptiles, and even creatures that have no feeling, to praise and love their Creator." Like the other panentheists we discussed in chapter 7, Francis was affirming the connection all creation shares to the Creator.

When Francis considered "all animals" as his brothers and sisters in God, he was also following the example of the ancient Celts, men and women of faith who had friendly relations with all sorts of creatures. According to legend, for example, Saint Brigid had as her companion since childhood a white, red-eared cow. (We also discussed Brigid earlier, in chapter 3.) She is often portrayed in religious art with her bovine friend. Some Saint Brigid stories may have roots in the older myths of the Goddess Brigid, since monks occasionally incorporated older stories into their tales of the saint. In any case, both Brigid the goddess and Brigid the saint were known for their affinities with the animal world.

One story tells that hunters were chasing a wild boar

and had nearly trapped it, when the boar ran into the enclosure of Saint Brigid's convent at Cill Dara. The huntsmen were forced to halt outside the gates and wait for the nuns to chase out the boar—but instead, Brigid sent out a message to the hunters, saying that the animal had the right of sanctuary in a convent, just as humans had. The hunters sent back a message protesting that animals don't have the same rights as human beings, so could they please have their boar back? Brigid responded that as far as she was concerned, the animal had the same right of sanctuary as people had—and that was that. As the disappointed hunters rode away, Brigid gave a drink to the exhausted and frightened animal, and then she led it to her own herd of pigs on the monastery farm. The boar soon became tame and settled in with the domestic pigs, where it lived happily for the rest of its life.

Another legend of Brigid concerns the king of Leinster's pet fox. The king had trained the fox to do tricks, and he loved it very much. One day, though, a workman saw the fox outside the palace and killed it, thinking that it was a wild animal. Passersby saw this deed, seized the man, and took him to the king. The king exploded with fury and grief, then ordered the workman's death.

When Brigid heard of this incident, in the words of her biographer Cogitosus, she "grieved in her inmost heart." She called for her chariot, jumped in, and thundered off toward the king's palace, praying as she went.

As the chronicle relates, "The Lord heard Brigid's cease-less prayers. He told a wild fox to come to her. The fox ran quickly across the plains to Brigid's chariot. It jumped nimbly up into the chariot and sat quietly under her cloak."

So Brigid came to the king and pleaded for the work-man's life. As she expected, the king refused, so she pro-duced the fox that had come to her en route to the palace. But the king was uninterested in a surrogate pet: his fox had been trained to do clever and unusual tricks; a wild fox would not delight him the same way. Then, to everyone's astonishment, Brigid gently requested that the wild fox do all the tricks the king required—and it did! Amazed, the king commanded that the workman be let go.

And there is more to the story. The wild fox had a mind of its own and did not want to be the king's pet. In Cogitosus's words:

> As Brigid was traveling home the fox weaved through the crowds, outwitted many horsemen and dogs and fled across the open plains and escaped unharmed to the wild desert places where his den was located.

And the result of all this? "All wondered at what had occurred. Brigid was venerated."

Lesser-known saints also had their creaturely compan-ions. According to one old Irish tale, when a slave girl left her newborn child to die on a forest hillside, a she-wolf found the infant boy and carried him to her lair, where she raised the man cub alongside her own. Eventually, a hunter found the young child and adopted him, giving him the name Ailbe. Perceiving God's hand in his unusual deliverance, Ailbe become a devoted Christ-follower, and in adulthood, he became the Bishop of Munster.

One day, he heard the sound of a wolf fleeing from hunters in the woods. He rushed to the scene and found the she-wolf who had reared him. Overwhelmed with joy at the chance to repay the creature, he took her into his home, where she spent the end of her days with Ailbe and his monks.

Kenneth (Coinneach, in Gaelic) was another saint known for his affinity with animals. Once when Coinneach was in the forest on a solitary religious retreat, a stag came to him and lowered its antlers to the ground before him. Coinneach set his gospel text on the deer's antlers as a book rest. The next day, the stag and Coinneach again met in the woods, and the deer again acted as a book rest for the saint. Day after day, the same thing happened, but one day, startled by a sudden noise, the deer dashed away, carrying the book still open on his antlers. Fortunately, the stag soon returned, with the book unharmed.

After reading all these wondrous—and possibly exaggerated!—tales of saints and their animal companions, it's nice to remember that the ancient Celts also had ordinary pets, which they enjoyed as we do ours. One such pet was Pangur Ban, immortalized in verse by his anonymous ninth-century Irish owner, a scribe. The scribe, like many other writers, knew the quiet sense of companionship a cat can offer while both writer and cat goes about his own business.

> I and Pangur Ban my cat,
> 'Tis a like task we are at:
> Hunting mice is his delight,
> Hunting words I sit all night.
>
> Better far than praise of men
> 'Tis to sit with book and pen;
> Pangur bears me no ill will,
> He too plies his simple skill.
>
> 'Tis a merry thing to see
> At our tasks how glad are we,
> When at home we sit and find
> Entertainment to our mind.
>
> Oftentimes a mouse will stray
> In the hero Pangur's way;
> Oftentimes my keen thought set
> Takes a meaning in its net.
>
> 'Gainst the wall he sets his eye
> Full and fierce and sharp and sly;
> 'Gainst the wall of knowledge I
> All my little wisdom try.

Furred and Feathered Neighbors

When a mouse darts from its den
O how glad is Pangur then!
O what gladness do I prove
When I solve the doubts I love!

So in peace our tasks we ply,
Pangur Ban, my cat, and I;
In our arts we find our bliss;
I have mine and he has his.

Practice every day has made
Pangur perfect in his trade;
I get wisdom day and night
Turning darkness into light.

Julian of Norwich, the fourteenth-century English mystic, would have likely echoed those sentiments. Julian was an anchoress who lived according to a Rule of Life that required she remain in a cell attached to a church. The cell had three windows: one into the church, one to communicate to a servant, and one that allowed her to speak to people in the outside world who came seeking her advice. She was allowed one companion inside her dwelling space—a cat, which kept mice and rats out of her quarters. Over the years of solitude, Julian must have grown close to her cat as they sat quietly together, settled in a contented state of mutual contemplation. Julian pondered her mystical visions, but what went through the cat's mind will forever remain a mystery (though it's probable that like Pangur Ban's pursuits, the cat's meditations were more mice-centered than mystical).

Love for animals is also visible in the artwork of the Celtic monks. Illuminated gospels like the Book of Kells swarm with creatures—salmon, eagles, peacocks, hounds, horses, cats, and even mice—all lovingly portrayed. Clearly, the Celts loved and appreciated the animal world.

These are touching stories. But what do they mean? What do they tell us about Celtic spirituality?

The Peaceable Kingdom
The Companionship of Creatures

Celtic Christians' love for animals had its roots in the pre-Christian Celtic world. A common pagan motif was transfiguration from human to animal forms, and a belief in this was carried into Celtic Christianity. In one old narrative, for instance, when Saint Finnen seeks out a chieftain, Tuan of Ulster, who is reputed to know the entire history of Ireland, Tuan reveals to the monk that he has witnessed the long history of the Isle in differing physical forms. First Tuan was human, but then he changed into the king of all the deer of Ireland. As one human race displaced another in Ireland, Tuan changed again; this time he became a wild boar. Again, civilizations rose and fell, and Tuan became an eagle. Finally, with the coming of the new faith, he was transformed again into a man. He relates his firsthand view—from various animal perspectives—of Ireland's history.

Such myths hearken back to the shamanistic practices of druidism. Like Merlin in the woods, Celtic sages sought to gain power and insight by associating with the skills, instincts, and special gifts of the animal world. Tales of shape-shifting might reflect such skillful practices as perceiving like a hawk, running through the forest with the agility of the deer, or swimming like the salmon. By means of meditation or entheogens (psychoactive natural substances), shamans could experience the powers of the animal world. The Gundestrup Cauldron, a pre-Christian Celtic artifact, portrays the horned god Cernunnos sitting in meditation, surrounded by all the creatures of the forest. This portrayal reflects the worldview of a Celtic sage, connected with the powers of the winged and feathered creatures around him.

If the older religion predisposed Celtic Christians toward affinity with the beasts, the Egyptian Mothers and Fathers of the Desert, whose legendary spiritual feats the Celts strove to emulate, influenced them just as much. An ancient bestselling book, *Lives of the Desert Fathers*, included a number of animal stories. This book, written late in the fourth century, is an eyewitness account of the writers' travels through the wilderness.

The book includes several descriptions of the Coptic hermits' fearlessness when it came to poisonous snakes. A group of monks told the writers, "We have . . . fulfilled in our own lives the Scripture which says, 'I gave unto you power to tread on serpents and scorpions, and over all the power of the enemy'" (Luke 10:19). (One wonders how many hermits may have perished in the desert sands, claiming this verse but finding their reaction time slower than their victorious snake-stomping brethren!)

A hermit named Amoun was said to have put a pair of serpents to good use when robbers kept breaking into his cave and stealing his meager fare. He went out into the desert, found two enormous venomous snakes, and bid them to follow him back to his dwelling place. The snakes slithered obediently after him and then remained outside the entrance to the hermit's abode, guarding against robbers—who promptly ceased troubling the holy man. Another Egyptian hermit, Abba Helle, was said to have tamed a crocodile that he trained to ferry him across a river.

Animal accounts in the *Lives of the Desert Fathers* emphasize the power of God in the Coptic believers' lives. The desert saints mastered beasts just as they overcame illnesses, starvation, and temptation. These stories served as living illustrations of Genesis 1:26, where God commanded humans "*Rule over* the fish of the sea and the birds of the air and over every living creature that moves on the ground" (emphasis mine).

Although both druids and Egyptians influenced the Celtic Christians, their relationships with animals differed from both. Unlike the shamans, Celtic Christians did not merge with the animals' consciousness or appropriate their attributes. And unlike the stories of the Desert Fathers, Celtic legends portray their heroes living alongside the animals, emphasizing commonality, respect, and tenderness rather than authority. So we must look elsewhere for the deepest spiritual meaning behind Celtic Christians' affinity with the creatures.

Ancient Celtic Christians perceived their relations with animals as signs of the Kingdom of God. The Celts who followed Christ believed they ushered this kingdom into existence whenever they brought the gospel to their lands. They understood the Kingdom of God as both a restoration of the past and portent of the future.

Friendly relations with the beasts are a reminder of the kingdom in its pristine state at the time of creation. In Genesis 2, Adam named all the animals as God created them and paraded them before him (19–20). Genesis gives us a picture of a peaceable world where God, humans, and beasts coexist harmoniously; it's a portrayal of life before humans fell into sin, dragging the entire world down with them.

At the same time, harmony among all creatures points to the Kingdom fully restored in the promised future. The Prophet Isaiah predicts a coming day when:

> *The wolf will live with the lamb,*
> *the leopard will lie down with the goat,*

the calf and the lion and the yearling together;
and a little child will lead them.
The cow will feed with the bear,
their young will lie down together,
and the lion will eat straw like the ox.
The infant will play near the hole of the cobra,
and the young child put his hand into the viper's nest.
They will neither harm nor destroy
on all my holy mountain,
for the earth will be full of the knowledge of the Lord
as the waters cover the sea. (11:6–9)

In this passage, the Kingdom of God reaches its fulfillment with the restoration of all things, including harmony between humans and beasts.

The early Christian Celts had a keen sense of living "between the times." While they respected their ancestors' spiritual ways, they also felt that the old ways were to a large extent darkened by ignorance. Early missionaries proclaimed, "The time has come, the Kingdom is near" (Mark 1:15), and they believed that their efforts were ushering in a new day of God's presence.

Soulish Beings
What Animals Can Teach Us

Adam said, "Lord, I am lonesome and have trouble remembering how much you love me."

God said, "No problem! I will create a companion for you so you will know my affection, even when you cannot see me. No matter how selfish and foolish you may be, this new companion will love you unconditionally, as I do."

So God created a new animal for Adam, and this new animal was so happy to be with the man, that it wagged its tail with joy.

But Adam said, "Lord, I do not have a name for the new animal."

And God said, "Because I created this animal to reveal my love for you, his name will have the same letters as my own name—you will call him Dog."

So Dog became Adam's best friend, and Dog was happy and wagged his tail even more.

But after a while, one of the angels complained to God, saying, "Lord, Adam has become arrogant. He is insufferably conceited. Dog has taught him that he is unconditionally loved—but no one teaches him humility.'

And the Lord said, "I have a solution! I will create another companion for him who will see the man as he is. This creature will remind him that he is not always worthy of adoration." And God created Cat.

Cat was certain he was far superior to Adam, and so Cat taught Adam humility. And God was pleased.

And Cat did not give a darn one way or the other.

This alternate take on the Genesis story has a meaning that goes deeper than just humor. Our pets can teach us a great deal about God and spiritual realities—if we are observant and open to their wisdom.

The ninth-century theologian John Scotus Erigena said, "The whole of reality . . . is God, since God is source, sustainer and end." He surmised this from the Apostle Paul who declared, "*in him* we live and move and have our being" (Acts 17:28). If all of nature—even inanimate things—reflects God, how much more should we see our Creator revealed in the animals, who are, according to the Hebrew Bible, "soulish beings" (the meaning of the Hebrew word *nephesh*, which is used to describe creatures)? While most theologians believe that animal souls differ from human souls—humans alone are made in God's image, they say—nonetheless, animals have a spiritual nature, and they have lessons to teach us about God.

The greatest Teacher of all used humans' relationships with animals to illustrate spiritual truth. When Jesus wanted to explain compassion he said:

> Suppose one of you has a hundred sheep and loses one of them. Does he not leave the ninety-nine in the open country and go after the lost sheep until he finds it? And when he finds it, he joyfully puts it on his shoulders and goes home. Then he calls his friends and neighbors together and says, "Rejoice with me; I have found my lost sheep." (Luke 15:3–6)

And when Christ needed an example of trust, he pointed to the birds:

> Therefore I tell you, do not worry about your life, what you will eat or drink; or about your body, what you will wear. Is not life more important than food, and the body more important than clothes? Look at the birds of the air; they do not sow or reap or store away in barns, and yet your heavenly Father feeds them. (Matthew 6:25–26)

A similar saying in Luke's gospel speaks specifically of ravens, those amazingly intelligent scavengers: "Consider the ravens: They do not sow or reap, they have no storeroom or barn; yet God feeds them" (Luke 12:24). I live adjacent to a field where large ravens are a daily sight. The great glossy birds never seem hurried or troubled; they just lounge around on poles or fences, keeping their sharp eyes open for the next meal—which humans or natural events always provide. Truly, God feeds the ravens.

But there's an additional level to Jesus' ravens allusion; it reminds us of another story in the Hebrew Bible, when a raven fed Elijah in the wilderness. Jewish rabbis see that story not just as an example of Divine provision but also as God's gentle chastisement of the prophet. Elijah had stopped the rain to punish Israel, rather than wooing the people with hope of God's forgiveness. While Elijah was bent on punishment, rather than mercy, the ravens were the Lord's messengers: if these birds fed Elijah, how much more should Elijah have "fed" the people of Israel and won them over to follow God? Within this context, we understand the words of Jesus with a new depth: if God provides for the ravens, He will surely provide all things for us—so we need not covet and grasp, but can freely share God's bounty with others. And if we have no worries for our own well-being, can we not—as Elijah should have—offer mercy to all? "Perfect love drives out fear" (1 John 4:8), and when perfect love has quelled our fears, then we too can love others more perfectly. All these deep spiritual lessons can be pulled out of the layers of trust between ravens and God, between a human and ravens, between that human and God, and between that human and other humans.

It's not surprising that Jesus used the creatures to teach his disciples; animals' instructional value was part of Israel's wisdom tradition. Job, the sage of ancient times, was aware of how we can gain knowledge from the animal world: "But ask the animals, and they will teach you, or the birds of the air, and they will tell you" (12:7).

The ancient Celtic saints followed the example of their Master, and they respected the contributions of their four-legged and winged friends to their spiritual lives. The Doctor Doolittle saints—Brigid, Columba, Francis of Assisi, and others—were real people, and while some of their exploits with animals may be exaggerated, actual events and attitudes underlie the tales.

Furred and Feathered Neighbors

The Celts' harmony with animals can be partially explained by the fact that their daily lives were much more attuned to their natural environment than our lives are today. Just like the animals around them, the Celts were dependent on rains, tides, vegetable growth, and the changing seasons; the animals were truly their brothers and sisters, experiencing the same reality humans did. Unlike the modern world, the ancient Celtic society produced few artificial noises—no shriek of cars and horns, no chug of machinery or blare of stereos to frighten away their woodland neighbors. The Celts relied more on instinct and intuition than we do, and they also focused their intellects to perceive subtle variations in the natural world that few of us would notice. Living close to the Earth, they felt a natural intimacy with their fellow creatures.

But we too can claim some of that intimacy, even in our twenty-first-century world, even in the "settled places" where many of us live. Years ago, for instance, when I was in college, I left my dormitory room at Michigan State University to be alone and pray in some woods adjacent to campus. It was nighttime, but a full moon provided adequate light so I could walk through the forest. I stopped beside a large fallen log and knelt on it, speaking in a soft whisper to God, assuming that none but the trees would hear me. After some time in prayer, I stopped and opened my eyes—and was astonished to see that a large raccoon stood up on its haunches, only a couple of feet away, with its forepaws leaning on the same tree. This is of course anthropomorphizing, but my immediate first impression was that the raccoon was praying just as I was. We stared at one another for a few minutes, and then he turned and disappeared into the brush. If this had happened in the Dark Ages and had been observed by another party, tales would have been told of "how Kenneth prayed in the forest with a wild raccoon"!

Some people—Brigid and Francis must have been like this—do have unusually strong capacities to understand animals. Dean Harrison and his wife Prayeri, owners of the Out of Africa Wildlife Park where they keep a number of big cats and other wild animals, seem, like the ancient saints, to have an innate propensity to relate with wildlife. In his book *Out of Eden*, Dean writes:

> When I was seven years old, the Lord gave me an instinct to see through the eyes of predators. That instinct has grown like a seed in the ground. And like the years it takes an oak to mature, that instinct has taken years to develop. It's primal, and it allows me to look from the predator's point of view. It permits "communication" and a sense of oneness with another, non-human individual."

As a result of this gift, combined with years of living in close proximity with cheetahs, lions, and tigers, Dean has described a set of insights that he describes as, "a new look at old relationships—man, animal and God."

FURRED AND FEATHERED NEIGHBORS

Regarding wild animals, humans tend to err in two opposite directions. On one extreme, we can anthropomorphize animals: act as if they are humans dressed up in furry guises. This can lead to dangerous mistakes, such as raising wild animals as "pets," forgetting that their behaviors and instincts are not at all human, and may in fact be potentially deadly. On the other extreme, philosophers and theologians may relegate nonhumans to "non-soulish" categories of existence, ignoring the fact that wild creatures do have unique personalities and exhibit advanced thinking and emotion. For example, wild animals have been observed on innumerable occasions grieving dead companions, especially mates. To learn what God will teach us through wild creatures, we must avoid both extremes, acknowledging both the profound differences between humans and animals, and also the complexities of animals' lives. This requires that we be humble enough to respect animals as being "other" than ourselves, creatures with their own unique behaviors and thought patterns.

The Harrisons have dedicated their lives to learning from wild animals—especially big cats—and sharing their insights with others. They treat these great creatures with respect, but they do not anthropomorphize them; in fact, they are keenly aware that wild cats can and do attack humans, even humans they are familiar with. Dean and Prayeri have many times been bitten or injured, despite their unparalleled knowledge of the big cats. But the Harrisons have learned that

As we watch the animals and the decisions they make, we realize that their life skills have application to our own lives. What is a good decision for them could be considered a good decision for us, for our families and our corporate and social activities.

Dean Harrison has written ninety-nine "principles of life," both practical and spiritual, based on their close relations with animals. The first principle is: "Obey the authority above you," a concept illustrated by the way water buffalo will follow the leader of its herd in order to survive. Dean writes, "In a broader sense, animals are completely obedient to their Creator. They live in perfect accord with the plan and purposes encoded within their species and for them as individuals." The second principle learned from close observation of wildlife? "Love your neighbor as yourself." The Harrisons draw this application from the fact that "when a lioness is being attacked by a pack of hyenas, her good deeds toward her companions will bring her help. But her inconsideration of others will leave her to defend herself, alone." Animals, the Harrisons have learned, have an innate, practical wisdom that can instruct human behavior as well.

Of course, you don't need to live in a wild animal park to learn from animals; like Adam in the humorous story at the beginning of this section, we can be abundantly blessed by knowing our dogs or cats. In my case, my good friend and close companion Duke, a Border Collie mix, has greatly enriched my life.

Duke was a rescue dog that had been abused by his original owner. When he first came into our home, he was afraid of me, though not so afraid of my wife—a reminder that his cruel first owner had been a male. He would hide from me, slinking into corners and under furniture. If I laughed suddenly or made a sudden move, Duke would cower and shake with fear. A long, nasty scar along his flank suggested the reason for this fear. He was such a beautiful, good-natured creature that we could not imagine how anyone had ever raised a hand to injure him.

As the months lengthened into our first year together, Duke gradually overcame his fear of me. He first decided to move his sleeping place from hiding under the furniture to a bed beside ours; then he began to take food from my hand; finally, he would rub up against me, asking to be pet. After several years, Duke was loyally and passionately attached to both my wife and me. Any time one of us came home, he would bark and run to the door, wagging his tail exuberantly. If I stayed home to write, he followed me around the house if I got up to get something and then sat beside me on the floor as I typed away at my desk. He lived to please; even a disapproving scowl from us would make him look crestfallen, and if we asked, "Want to take a walk?" he would practically explode with barking and prancing enthusiasm.

Duke died while I was writing this book, but I continue to reflect on Duke's truly limitless loyalty and love. We had redeemed him from a brutal master—though our act of redemption brought us as much joy as it did him—and he gave himself to us unreservedly in return, up until his last hour of life. Should we not give ourselves just as freely to Christ, who redeemed us at a much more costly price? I find great joy in thinking that our affection for God brings as much Divine delight as Duke's companionship brought us.

Duke's death was a painful blow to me. Perhaps the last lesson he needed to teach me was to let go and trust God with the final destiny of a dear friend and constant companion. Even now, writing these words, I have to stop and wipe tears from my eyes.

Shortly after Duke died, a friend who cares for rescue dogs wrote me these consoling words: "Duke thanks you for a wonderful life and for being there when he needed you the most. Now he sits at God's feet, sharing all his memories of his great life and family with all in heaven." The image of Duke at God's feet is wonderfully comforting, but a skeptic might pause to ask, "Is that really true?"

Many theologians would say no, animals do not get to enjoy eternal life. The Bible doesn't say. There is only one passage in Judeo-Christian scripture that speaks of eternal salvation for animals, and that passage is agnostic on the issue:

I also thought, "As for men, God tests them so that they may see that they are like the animals. Man's fate is like that of the animals; the same fate awaits them both: As one dies, so dies the other.

All have the same breath; man has no advantage
over the animal. Everything is meaningless. All go
to the same place; all come from dust, and to dust
all return. Who knows if the spirit of man rises
upward and if the spirit of the animal goes down
into the earth?" (Ecclesiastes 3:18–21)

Celtic theologians, however, reached a different conclusion. John Scotus Erigena (Charlemagne's Irish-born
theologian) and C. S. Lewis (also born in Ireland, though
many centuries later) both wrote about animal salvation,
and both shared a similar view. Lewis and Erigena suggest that we are our pets' redeemers; our love for them
is a part of God's restoration of all things. Erigena writes,
"When man is recalled into the original grace of his nature
. . . he will gather again to himself every sensible creature
below him through the wonderful might exercised by the
Divine Power in restoring man." In Lewis's novel *The Great
Divorce*, he describes a "great lady" in heaven, surrounded
by a small menagerie, and he explains, "Every beast and
bird that came near her had its place in her love. In her
they became themselves. And now the abundance of life
she has in Christ from the Father flows over into them." On
a more humorous note, Robert Louis Stevenson writes,
"You think dogs will not be in heaven? I tell you, they will
be there long before any of us."

Some of the most ancient Christian theologians also
recognized that the animal world points to the heavenly

kingdom. They understood that by paying attention to this deep connection between the Spirit and the beasts, we can find practical applications to our own lives. Saint Jerome, the fourth-century church father, wrote:

> We marvel at the Creator, not only as the one who made heaven and earth, sun and ocean, elephants, camels, horses, oxen, leopards, bears and lions, but also as the one who made the small creatures: ants, gnats, flies, worms and the like—things whose shape we know better than their names. And as in all creation we revere his skill, so the one whose mind is given to Christ is earnest in small things as in great, knowing that an account must be given even for an idle word.

Nine centuries later, Anthony of Padua, one of the followers of Saint Francis of Assisi who had been influence by Celtic spirituality, described a similar perspective:

> Our thoughts ought by instinct to fly upwards from animals, men, and natural objects to their creator. If created things are so utterly lovely, how gloriously beautiful must he be who made them! The wisdom of the worker is revealed in his handiwork.

Every day of your mortal life, you are surrounded by blessings, even on the days when all is not well, and you are ill or troubled. The animals around you are among these blessings, sure signs of Divine grace, for the scriptures affirm that God sends the Divine waters for the animals as much as for humans, for all alike reflect the Lord's glory. The wonder of the Divine plan is revealed in the amazing intricacy of the animal kingdom, and God has put the four-footed and winged ones in our lives for a reason.

Wild creatures live according to their own designs, allowing us a glimpse of their routines only when they please, and our pets, alas, have shorter lives than we do. So pay attention when your fellow creatures share their lives with you. Watch closely. Listen carefully. Open your heart. Let God speak to you through these furred and feathered neighbors.

Lord God,
make my heart straight in your sight,
so that every creature will be to me a mirror of life,
and a book of holy doctrine.
For there is no creature
so small or insignificant
that it does not show forth and represent
the goodness of God.
—Thomas à Kempis

Every creature is a divine word because it proclaims God.
—Saint Bonaventure

The Celts' love of animals was expressed in their artwork, where
birds and beasts twined together with endless knots, expressing
the interweaving unity of all life.

9
WATER INTO WINE
SIGNS AND WONDERS

A wedding took place at Cana in Galilee. Jesus' mother was there, and Jesus and his disciples had also been invited to the wedding. When the wine was gone, Jesus' mother said . . . to the servants, "Do whatever he tells you." Nearby stood six stone water jars. . . . Jesus said to the servants, "Fill the jars with water." . . . Then he told them, "Now draw some out and take it to the master of the banquet." . . . The master of the banquet tasted the water that had been turned into wine . . . and said, "Everyone brings out the choice wine first and then the cheaper wine after the guests have had too much to drink; but you have saved the best till now." This, the first of his miraculous signs, Jesus performed in Cana of Galilee.
—John 2:1–4, 6–11

"You there, lad!"

Gelefed ignored the man who called his name. He was used to insults and jests, so he just shuffled along with his head down. Even if someone actually wished to speak with him, it wouldn't make any difference: he was unable to speak a word in reply. He had been dumb since birth.

"I say, boy!" The man was insistent.

Gelefed turned and peered at the man. The coarse grey habit and the copper cross that hung on the man's chest told Gelefed he was a monk from the nearby monastery at Inderauuda. Gelefed raised his hand in a sign of recognition. Sometimes, when his family had nothing to eat, he would enter the stone wall of the monks' community, point to his stomach, and plead with his eyes. Even though the monks appeared to have little of their own, he always left the enclosure with a loaf of bread or some fresh-picked vegetables.

"You're Gelefed, aren't you?" the man asked.

The young man nodded and pulled his knit cap down tighter on his head; he was always afraid it would fall off, exposing the huge scabs that afflicted his scalp.

"I'm brother Berhthun," the monk said. "Our holy bishop, John, has retreated to a little hermitage in the woods not far from here to pray and read Holy Scripture during this season of Lent."

Gelefed looked at the monk, uncomprehending.

"It is the season that our blessed Lord Jesus went to Jerusalem, to die and rise again."

The teenager's eyes showed no sign of caring or understanding, so the monk persisted. "Every Lent, we ask one of the villagers to join us for our holy vigil—and this year, Abbot John asked me to summon you."

Now Gelefed's eyes widened slightly.

"If you'll come and be our guest, we'll be happy to share our fare with you, and to pray for . . . your welfare."

The young man's eyes darted back and forth, and the monk realized he was uncertain as to what he should do.

"If you'd like to come with me and share our abode in the woods, just nod yes."

The boy's face was blank, but his head moved up and down.

"Very good. I'm going to buy some fish, and then I'll speak with your family for their permission. Right then, let's be getting along."

Over the next few days, Gelefed became accustomed to the ways of the holy men with their odd customs. Back home, his father left offerings for a figure holding a rude hammer made from a wooden post, which represented Thor. When things went badly, Gelefed's father would yell and then cry before the statue, trying to cajole its response. Gelefed was fairly sure the statue was no more likely to respond than his own useless tongue was. But these monks made no offerings; their only tangible object of devotion was a stone cross where the four brothers would gather for long hours, listening to readings from an enormous book or chanting prayers in unison. Gelefed had never seen anyone read before, and the way the monks would stare at the parchment and speak rapidly, as if the book transmitted words into their heads, seemed magical to him.

Gelefed liked being with these strange people, though he was careful to keep his face expressionless. At home, his family was embarrassed by his silence and disgusted by his sores. But the monks addressed him—and each other—in gentle voices. They treated him like an honored guest, something he'd never experienced before.

On the third day, while Gelefed was sitting on a log watching the monks at prayer, Bishop John walked over and joined him. The bishop was a tall man with chiseled features and a wispy beard. His features seemed young, but the holy man's eyes were full of wisdom, like the old shaman's in Gelefed's village.

Bishop John knelt directly in front of the boy. "Can I pray for you, son?"

Gelefed's eyes said, *Yes.*

"Stick out your tongue."

The lad hesitated, then did so.

The bishop pulled a flask filled with holy water from his robes, sprinkled a few drops on his hand, then made the sign of a cross with his wet finger on Gelefed's tongue. "All right then—say something," the holy man requested.

Gelefed looked like a deer trapped by hunters; had all this kindness been simply another trick to humiliate him?

But Bishop John was insistent, his voice firm though kind. "In the name of Jesus, Gelefed, say something. Say, *gae!*" (*Gae* was the Saxon word for "yes.")

"G–g–ga . . . ga—" The young man was perspiring, shaking, as if pouring his entire soul into the effort.

"Ga–gae. Gae. Gae!" The third time, he shouted, shaking from head to toe with joy and excitement.

"Ah, that's fine, lad. That's wonderful, that is! See, you can speak now." The bishop clasped his shoulder. "Now let's start on the alphabet. The first letter is 'a.' Say 'a'— like this . . ."

The rest of that afternoon and into the evening, Bishop John helped Gelefed recite sound after sound. The boy grew more exuberant with each new pronunciation. The other monks gathered around, whispering among themselves as they watched the young man's first speech.

The bishop and his new pupil continued their exchange for the remainder of the holy season. After a week, Gelefed could say words. Within another week, he could make baby sentences. And by the third week, he was talking nonstop, his words shooting out like a geyser. The monks whispered among themselves that it was a sign from God. Surely, they told each other, they had beheld just as great a proof of God's miraculous power as the miracles wrought in the days of the apostles.

The morning after Palm Sunday, Bishop John told Gelefed to pack a lunch and put on his cloak.

"W–why, John? Do I have to . . . go now?" The boy's tone and expression betrayed his fear.

The bishop shook his head. "There is a hermit who lives a few miles from here, a holy man who prays to Christ and practices herb lore. It's time we took care of your skin disease."

The young man shrank back and pulled his cap down tighter over his head, terrified at the thought of exposing the raw wounds for scrutiny.

The bishop looked him in the face. "Did God not deliver you from dumbness? Do you not pour forth speech now, due to the mercies of the Lord?"

"Yes, Father, I do."

"Then why not trust God to heal your skin, as well? The Lord wants you to be fully healed."

Gelefed agreed. He and the bishop made the journey to visit the herbalist, who prescribed a treatment that soon healed the scabs that had plagued Gelefed for so long.

Sometime later, after Easter had come and gone, Gelefed strode back into his village. A pretty girl, who used to avert her eyes from him, stared openly as he made his way down the dirt road between the huts.

"Have I seen you before?" she asked.

Gelefed grinned. "Hello, Frigga. It's me, Gelefed."

"Gelefed? No! You're joking."

He laughed.

"But—" She pointed at the long, curling locks of yellow hair that tumbled down from his head. "And—" This time she pointed at his mouth.

Gelefed shrugged. "Aye, I can talk now. And I'm healed. God has done a miracle for me, through the bishop and the other brothers."

Frigga wanted to ask all about what had happened—but she was interrupted by the villagers who came running and shouting to see the boy who'd been so amazingly restored.

Wonders and Miracles
Signs of God's Presence in the World

This dramatized account of a boy's healing is adapted from Bede's *Ecclesiastical History*. It's one in a series of accounts concerning John of Hexham, an early missionary to the Saxons. Bede says, "Many miracles were told of him by those who knew him well and especially by the most reverend and truthful Berhthun, once his deacon."

Most of us have at one time or another wished for a miracle in our lives. Our struggles often feel like more than we can handle, so we hope for supernatural intervention equal to the enormous challenges we face. At the same time, we may be skeptical of the reality of supernatural aid. In our modern world, "miracle workers" are often scamming someone—and the only "real" miracles are the result of science's advances.

The Celtic Christians and their neighbors were convinced that miracles were real, however. Their ancestors had lived in a world they considered enchanted, peopled by nature spirits, ghosts, banshees, and fairies. These mythical denizens of the Gaelic lands live on, even today, in the folklore of Ireland, Scotland, and Wales. Entering an ancient barrow or wandering through an old oak grove will make you half-believe the tales of pixies and wee folk!

The Celts also believed in the powers of supernatural springs—and that belief lingers on in the Isles as well, where people still visit holy wells to pray, drink healing water, and leave "clooties" (articles of clothing) for blessing. The idea of healing wells was not unique to Celts either. The Gospel of John notes two pools in Jerusalem—Siloam and Bethesda—where miraculous healings occurred.

The Christian Celts' druidic ancestors gifted them with a supernatural perspective, while we, on the other hand, are children of the scientific revolution. We can't help but turn a skeptical eye toward many of the exaggerated elements in the stories of the Celtic saints. I find it hard to believe, for instance, that Saint Winifred was beheaded, then picked up her lovely head and placed it back on her shoulders. I suspect, however, that many of the mediaeval chroniclers didn't believe such tales, either. They were simply good stories, with plenty of entertainment value.

In contrast to such exaggerated legends, though, are saints' lives that are carefully documented. Bede assures us in the preface to his history, "I . . . made it my business to add with care what I was able to learn myself from the trustworthy testimony of reliable witnesses." Especially when he recounts the signs and wonders done by believers, Bede strove to give the actual names and locations of witnesses and events, anticipating the skepticism of his readers. Likewise, many of the miracles in the *Lives of the Desert Fathers* are firsthand accounts by the writers, who anticipated a skeptical audience and strove for veracity. Christians in the fourth through the eighth centuries in Egypt and in the British Isles may have truly experienced some amazing events.

If there's one thing the four Gospels agree on it is this: Jesus did miracles—a whole lot of miracles. Later, the Desert Mothers and Fathers and the Celtic Christians believed that they would likewise experience signs and wonders in their midst. But can we extrapolate from their experiences that we should expect miracles today?

First, though, let's take a moment to define terms. What constitutes a miracle? Perhaps the worst definition is Tertullian's, who defined a miracle as something "to be believed because it is absurd." Thomas Aquinas later provided a definition still common today, that a miracle is any event "outside the order of nature." Unfortunately, that definition paved the way for philosophical attacks on the possibility of miracles by David Hume and other skeptics. Hume stated that in order for a miracle to be believed genuine, it would have to be witnessed by enough credible witnesses to outweigh the number of people who had witnessed the "natural" course of events—and, Hume insisted, there are *no* human beings who are 100 percent credible, so this requirement can never be met.

In contrast with Aquinas, however, C. S. Lewis argued that miracles are *not* contrary to nature. Lewis wrote that God does "the very same things" in miracles that happen in nature, but "at a different speed and on a smaller scale." As examples, Lewis compares Christ's miracles with God's usual activities in nature:

> God creates the vine and teaches it to draw up water by its roots and, with the aid of the sun, to turn that water into a juice which will ferment and take on certain qualities. Thus every year . . . God turns water into wine.

God did the same thing at an unusually quick speed when Christ turned water into wine at Cana. Likewise, Lewis said, God is constantly at work healing people, usually through the body's own slow capacity to heal—but in Christ, God chose to heal people almost instantly.

A statement presented by theologians at Fuller Theological Seminary emphasizes that we always live in a "God-permeated cosmos," and therefore, "a miracle is not a sign that a God who is usually absent is, for the moment, present. It is only a sign that God who is always present in creative power is working here and now in an unfamiliar style."

Likewise, some modern philosophers categorize miracles as part of "the unknown." Science cannot fathom all the mysteries in the universe, and miracles may simply be events that science cannot explain adequately, given our present understanding. Imagine if the ancient Celts could see a cell phone; they would very likely consider it either magical or miraculous!

WATER INTO WINE

The New Testament has a different point of view on miracles: they are not something mysterious so much as they are signs of a deeper reality. A miracle's significance is not that it is astounding or mystifying but that it points to God. A biblical "sign" could be as extraordinary as the Red Sea parting for Moses or as ordinary as a spectacular sunset. From this perspective, a miracle is anything that powerfully indicates the presence of God.

The ancient Celts were so familiar with miraculous signs that they created a taxonomy of such wonders. The categories of supernatural events can be seen in the title of a seventh-century biography, *The Prophecies, Miracles, and Visions of St. Columba (Columcille)*. Adamnan, Columba's successor as abbot at Iona, wrote this biography that lists almost a hundred supernatural events, all divided into those three types.

The first sort of "sign" is prophecy or clairvoyance. Columba proved an especially gifted seer when lives were at stake. Three times he narrated to his disciples battles that were being fought far away. Likewise, he was able to anticipate guests to the island well before their vessels came into sight, telling his monks the names of travelers en route. Today we might consider that Columba had some form of extrasensory perception.

The second sort of "signs" in the Celtic taxonomy was what Adamnan calls "miracles," and these refer to changes in physical matter. These can be further divided into two types: first, healings of diseases, and second, control over natural forces.

As an example of the first sort, through his gift of seeing-at-a-distance, Columba knew that a nun across the waters in Ireland had broken her hip and lay moaning in pain. So he blessed a container of holy water and sent a messenger to the injured nun. According to the messenger's statement, the suffering lady bathed her hip with the holy water and was at once cured.

Another of Columba's healing miracles fits into the modern category of marriage counseling. On Rechrean Island, a man asked the saint to do something about his wife who was so vexed with him that she refused to go to bed with him. Columba spoke with the woman, who begged to be admitted to a convent rather than endure physical intimacy with her husband. Apparently, she was so disillusioned with her husband that he was no longer physically attractive to her. Hearing this, Columba invited both husband and wife to fast and pray with him through that night. They agreed to do so—and in the morning, after the conclusion of their prayer vigil, the wife was overcome with amorous desire for her husband. For the remainder of their earthly lives, the happy couple enjoyed all the pleasures of marriage. Those who have attempted marriage counseling can attest to the difficulty of achieving such a quick and thorough healing!

Along with healings of various sorts, Columba performed miracles that controlled the forces of nature. On one occasion, for example, he had retreated alone into a forest on the Isle of Skye, in order to meditate. As he prayed, he was disturbed by a clamor and looked up in time to see an enormous wild boar, pursued by hunters, headed straight toward him. The saint made the sign of a cross, and the boar fell dead in its tracks. (I can't help but contrast this with Brigid's miraculous rescue of the wild boar pursued by hunters. Even in the nature of their miracles, the unique personalities of the Celtic saints come through!)

Sometimes, Gaelic miracles took the form of maledictions. Columba was furious when he encountered a druid who was maltreating a female slave, and he sternly commanded the druid to let the young woman go. The magician scoffed at Columba's demand—and shortly after, the druid became deathly ill. He then released the girl and begged Columba's favorable prayer. Columba's word restored the druid to health.

In addition to prophecies and physical miracles, Columba experienced a third category of miracles: visions. Several of these were of "divine" or "heavenly" light, but most were visits from angels (the subject of the next chapter). The experience of John the Revelator that inspired the Book of Revelation would be an example of this kind of miracle, and countless saints have also experienced supernatural glimpses into the spiritual world.

The Hebrew and Christian scriptures and the records of the Celts are replete with miracles. According to David

Allan Hubbard, former president of Fuller Theological Seminary, "Miracles do not occur evenly throughout the course of salvation history . . . but they come in batches at times selected by God." They certainly came in quite a large batch at the time when Christianity was first entering the British Isles—but can you and I hope to experience such signs and wonders today?

Another Dimension
Miracles Today?

I cannot lay claim, personally, to any verifiable miracles, yet I have seen what I regard as astonishing answers to prayer. A family member received dramatic and sudden recovery from serious medical threats on two occasions, following intense sessions of prayer. However, a skeptic would brand these as "unlikely but not impossible coincidences." Spontaneous remissions of disease are rare, but they do not contradict science, and it could just be "luck" that such unusual events occurred when coupled with prayer. So my own experiences illustrate the difficulty of proving the miraculous. Many of us experience events that astonish us and—seen with eyes of faith—these events testify to God's power. Yet miracles by their very nature seem to defy documentation of the sort that skeptics demand.

Theologian Kenton Sparks points out that "human traditions from every time, place, and culture bear testimonies of miraculous events . . . the human perception that there is another dimension of reality, to some extent distinct from our own, is a widespread phenomenon." He concludes, "The hypothesis that a sacred realm exists, and that it will eventually intervene in human life, offers a better account—dare I say, a far better account—of the evidence than any secular account can."

Regarding the numerous miracle accounts in the Bible and in the lives of the ancient saints, we should not be embarrassed to follow the common sense of Thomas Reid (Scottish philosopher and contemporary of David Hume), who reminds us, "It is the very nature of human testimony—of a claim about the historical past—that it is more often true than not." Granted, extraordinary claims require uncommon proofs to be accepted. But at what point do claims cease to be extraordinary? A hundred claims? A thousand claims? Accounts of miracles and other supernatural events are far more common than that. Why not believe them on the same basis that we believe other aspects of human existence?

Over the past four years, I have taught comparative religion to hundreds of students at a nearby college. As part of my course, I elicit the students' personal experiences—or lack thereof—with the supernatural. Students' papers on this topic are wholly confidential. I find that a surprising number of students—about one in three—have experienced events that challenge ordinary explanation. Often, these involve life-saving circumstances or consolation in trying times. Students will rarely (almost never) share these aloud in class, but they are often anxious to discuss them privately; the events are important to them, and they lack an outlet where their perceptions are treated seriously. Curiously, students who report such events are not necessarily from religious backgrounds.

In the Bible, God's powers are not limited to those who follow Yahweh. (Balaam in the Book of Numbers is clearly a pagan sorcerer, who nonetheless prophesies by the power of the Israelite God.) So the ancient Celtic Christians were not surprised to see God's miracles amid those who did not acknowledge Christ, although they believed that God worked especially among those who followed Jesus.

In my classes, I am also fascinated by many students who are agnostic about God and yet have nevertheless experienced what can only be called a miracle—and then go to considerable lengths to explain away their experiences. I've known people who experienced a life-saving premonition or some sort of contact with an invisible being, and then later framed these events as the products of emotion or an unreliable memory. These same people, however, don't regard themselves as unreliable when remembering ordinary events.

So my interactions with people over the years convince me that C. S. Lewis was right when he said, "Whatever experiences we may have, we shall not regard them as miraculous if we already hold a philosophy which excludes the supernatural." In other words, miracles must be believed to be seen. Lewis pointed out that "miracles . . . appear to cease in Western Europe as materialism becomes the popular creed" simply because people are less prone to report them. But, he wrote, if people are receptive to "some reality beyond nature," then "accounts of the supernatural meet us on every side."

Many medical doctors admit improbable—even inexplicable—healings, although they are loath to call these "miracles," since the word implies religious commitments. Larry Dossey, M.D., in *Explore: The Journal of Science and Healing*, writes, "The phenomenon, referred to in medical literature as spontaneous remission, occurs when serious, often deadly illnesses such as cancer quickly and inexplicably—some would even say miraculously—disappear. No one knows exactly how often such cases occur. Approximately 3,500 medically documented cases of seeming miracles—based on reports from doctors in America and around the world dating to 1967—have appeared in 800 peer-reviewed medical journals and cover all major illnesses, including cancer, heart disease, diabetes and arthritis."

Are you comfortable with a reality beyond your understanding that could cause what seem to be supernatural events in your own life?

Leaving Room for Divine Mysteries
A Flexible Faith

God gives no promises of miraculous intervention. Some modern Christian groups urge believers to "name and claim" miracle healings in every case of illness or suffering. People with such beliefs must then blame the victim's "lack of faith" in cases where the victim fails to receive healing. I knew a man with this sort of belief whose wife was dying of cancer. He refused to accept that reality, always insisting, "God is healing her—but Satan has blinded the doctors, so her recovery will be even more glorious." When his wife died, he was devastated. I wished for him a more flexible faith, one that could have prepared himself and his beloved for her great transition into the next life.

In contrast with this dogmatic rigidity, the ancient saints knew that God works mysteriously. At times miracles come entirely unbidden, yet by the same token, a much-desired rescue might not occur. Brigid, Patrick, and Columba worked countless miracles, and yet they were prone to illnesses, injuries, the frailties of old age, and eventually, death. Celtic faith insisted that God is a great Mystery, even to those who know the Divine One best. God's creative action flows into the world in unpredictable ways.

Jesus promised that his followers would do the works he did and even greater ones as well (John

14:12–14). Does that mean we should always expect extraordinary healings? I don't pretend to know for certain what Jesus meant, but I think it's reasonable to suppose that the achievements of modern technology fulfill Jesus' promise. When you consider the millions of lives saved by vaccines, by restorative surgery, by preventive care, and by advanced agricultural technologies that feed people who would otherwise starve, it seems that science and human compassion have indeed done "greater works" than the miracles Jesus himself performed. So, when seeking God's wonder-working power, we should embrace and celebrate the medicines, doctors, and technology God has given us, and expect God to work through these ordinary yet almost-miraculous means. The ancient Celts, with their holistic view of life and spirituality, celebrated "God healing" through doctors or through miracles, with equal acclaim for both. Note that in the story of Gelefed, the bishop healed the young man's speech problems with prayer alone, but he then relied on a healer's remedies to cure Gelefed's skin condition.

We must also recognize that "healing" may mean different things. For a person suffering with protracted illness (physical or mental), death may be a more glorious healing than any recovery to a "normal" earthbound state. With our mortal limitations, we suffer grief when our friends and loved ones are taken from us, but most of us are not so selfish or so skeptical that we fail to believe

that those who have departed are in a far happier state.
In all the biographies of Celtic saints, the day of death
marks the entry to the blessed realms, the glorious com-
pletion of life.

At the same time, prayer for healing and deliverance
from our woes is a God-approved aspect of our life on
Earth. Jesus' brother James wrote, "You have not because
you ask not" (4:2). The Christian scriptures overflow with
incentives to prayer rooted in the conviction that "all
things are possible with God."

In the lives of the Celtic saints, a connection is apparent between sanctity and supernatural power, between
commitment to knowing God and having access to Divine
power. This tie between contemplation and miracles is
obvious in the biographies of the Celtic saints and those
of the Desert Mothers and Fathers. On Irish skelligs and
the dry caves in the Egyptian desert, these followers of
Christ doggedly pursued "the single eye" directed toward
God. The Divine voice was more familiar to some of
them than the sounds of their mortal companions, and
they often heard it prompt them toward supernatural ministry. In the prologue to the *Lives of the Desert
Fathers*, the author points out the "stillness" of the Coptic
saints' lives and goes on to explain:

> when one of them lacks something necessary, he
> does not go to a town or village, or to a brother, or
> friend or relation . . . to procure what he needs,

for his will alone is sufficient. When he raises his hands to God in supplication . . . all these things are provided for him in a miraculous way.

So if we desire supernatural empowerment, the wisdom of the Celts points us to the spiritual practices that help us to see God more clearly, such as noticing the Divine Presence in ordinary life, spending time alone in contemplation, and the disciplines of green martyrdom, all of which are detailed in other chapters of this book.

Another obvious requirement for experiencing the supernatural world is prayer. Intercession is the river that carries Divine power in its current. Jesus used all sorts of metaphors to communicate the amazing power of intercession: prayer beats down the gates of hell, moves mountains, and (when practiced by Jesus) raises the dead to life. The poet Tennyson spoke true when he placed these words in the mouth of the dying King Arthur:

> More things are wrought by prayer than this world dreams of. . . . For what are men better than sheep or goats that nourish a blind life within the brain, if, knowing God, they lift not hands of prayer both for themselves and those who call them friend? For so the whole round earth is every way bound by gold chains about the feet of God.

C. S. Lewis, in his essay titled "Work and Prayer," cited Pascal's idea that God gave mortals "the dignity of causality" for events in the universe. Lewis then goes on to explain that this "dignity of causality" is expressed by two means: physical actions and prayers. Though we ordinarily think of these two ways as being quite different, Lewis insists that "both are alike in this respect—that in both we try to produce a state of affairs which God has not seen fit to provide on his own." He adds that work and prayer differ, inasmuch as God retains veto power over prayer, for "had he not done so, prayer would be an activity too dangerous for man."

Theologian Walter Wink says of prayer:

> It creates an island of relative freedom in a world gripped by an unholy necessity. . . . A space opens in the praying person, permitting God to act without violating human freedom. The change in even one person thus changes what God can thereby do in that world.

He concludes, "By means of our intercessions we veritably cast fire upon the earth and trumpet the future into being."

If Lewis and Wink are correct, then prayer erases the dichotomy between "natural" and "supernatural" events. To put it in ancient Celtic terms, prayers create "thin spots" where the visible and invisible realms pass back and forth.

The praying man or woman can say with Moses, "Do not be afraid. Stand firm and you will see the deliverance the LORD will bring you today" (Exodus 14:13).

Miracles thrive amid the spiritual disciplines and earnest prayer. These activities generate a strong and healthy faith, and normally, faith is a prerequisite for miracles. But how do we generate faith? We cannot, to quote *Alice in Wonderland,* "believe six impossible things before breakfast." How do we summon faith in the face of our fears and doubts?

When the disciples were puzzled by their inability to work a miracle in his name, Jesus told them their lack of faith was the problem. "For truly I tell you, if you have faith the size of a mustard seed, you will say to this mountain, 'Move from here to there,' and it will move; and nothing will be impossible for you" (Matthew 17:20). Jesus' hyperbolic saying is encouraging. You don't need a huge faith or a perfect faith, just enough to give God a start in the situation; then God can do "more than we ask or imagine according to this power that is at work within us" (Ephesians 3:20).

Our faith will also grow as we follow the Celtic Christians' example and learn to see the miraculous nature of everyday reality. Priest Michael Mitton, writing of the visions experienced by the Celts, explains, "The training ground for such visions was learning to see and hear God *through his creation on earth*" (italics mine). This goes along with C. S. Lewis's belief, mentioned earlier in this chapter, that when miracles occur, God does "the very same things" that God does in nature, but "at a different speed and on a smaller scale."

This means you have already seen miracles in the "natural" world—you just don't always recognize them as such. Think about it, though. Isn't it astounding that each person you know began as a microscopic set of cells in a womb, and then grew from infancy to old age, changing every day yet remaining one person? The more you explore the world, the more amazing things you will see. When you see a whale leap out of the ocean beside your boat . . . survey a vast mountain range from its peak . . . or watch a volcano erupt—in moments like that, you cannot doubt that God is the author of miracles.

The connection between miracles and nature struck me recently when a medieval vision and a modern science documentary merged. I was reading Julian of Norwich's *Showings* and came to her famous passage in which she describes how God showed her "something small, no bigger than a hazelnut, lying in the palm of my hand, as it seemed to me, and it was round as a ball." Julian asks God "What can this be?" And the response is, "It is everything which is made." That evening, I was watching a television program about the beginnings of the cosmos. Using special effects, the show portrayed the beginning of everything—all the matter that now exists in the vast universe—collapsed into what they described as "a sphere smaller than a marble." Perhaps

WATER INTO WINE

God showed Julian in the Middle Ages a miraculous picture, one that science now substantiates: the infinite cosmos—everything that is made—*did* originate in a ball the size of a hazelnut.

If you can believe that, then you can generate faith the size of a mustard seed—and you'll begin to see your own miracles. Remember, though, that miracles are simply signs of God's presence. They don't need to be sensational; sometimes, the Divine Presence is revealed in something as small—and miraculous—as a baby's first laugh or an old woman's smile. God knows exactly what you need.

Trust God to turn the waters of your life into fine wine.

Let him who will laugh and insult,
I will not be silent,
nor will I hide the signs and wonders
which were ministered to me by the Lord
—Saint Patrick

*The ancient Celts believed the world was filled with "thin places,"
where a human could stick his head through into the heavenly
realm. Miracles and wonders were more likely to
occur in these places.*

10
BEINGS OF LIGHT AND DARKNESS
ANGELS AND DEMONS

The angel of the LORD found Hagar
near a spring in the desert.
—Genesis 16:7

Are not all angels ministering spirits
sent to serve those who will inherit salvation?
—Hebrews 1:14

Once long, long ago, a slave master forced a woman of African descent to bear his child. Like a mare or a cow, she was valued only for her ability to produce offspring. But in the midst of her suffering, pregnant and abandoned, she received an amazing message brought to her by an angel.

The woman's name was Hagar, and her story is told in the Hebrew Bible. "You are now with child," the angel tells her, "and you will have a son. You shall name him Ishmael ['God hears'] for the Lord has heard of your misery." Genesis chapter 16 adds that Hagar "gave this name to the Lord who spoke to her: "You are the God who sees me." From her culture's perspective, Hagar was invisible, a throwaway person—and yet she was important enough to God that a Divine messenger came to let her know she was both seen and heard.

All this took place at a specific, recognizable place—"the spring that is beside the road to Shur"—a fact that the scripture author includes matter-of-factly, assuming his readers will recognize the place. The juxtaposition of a familiar location and an angelic appearance may startle modern readers. We think of angels appearing in spangled hazy dreams—rather than standing, say, on the corner of Broad Street and Main, in front of Starbucks.

But the Celtic saints were as comfortable as the biblical heroes were with the presence of angels in their lives. As late as the seventeenth century, Scottish Presbyterian minister Samuel Rutherford claimed that when he was a child, an angel pulled him out of a well into which he had fallen. The Bible affirms that angels are one of the ways God refreshes our spirits.

"It was not Christmas; it was not even wintertime, when the event occurred that for me threw sudden new light on the ancient angel tale." That's how S. Ralph Harlow, who was professor of Religion and Biblical Studies at Smith College in Northampton, Massachusetts, began his account of something that many of his academic peers would find preposterous: a sighting of angels. Dr. Harlow knew the incredulity that would greet his account, so he gave his credentials as a reliable witness.

What can I say about myself? That I am a scholar who shuns guesswork and admires scientific investigation? That I have an A.B. from Harvard, an M.A. from Columbia, and a Ph.D. from Hartford Theological Seminary? That I have never been subject to hallucinations? That attorneys have solicited my testimony and I have testified in the courts as a faithful reliable witness? All this is true, and yet I doubt any amount of credentials can influence the belief or disbelief of another.

Dr. Harlow went on to relate that he and his wife, Marion, on a May walk in the Massachusetts woods heard voices apparently coming from above them. Looking up, they saw:

about ten feet above us and slightly to our left was a floating group of glorious beautiful creatures that glowed with spiritual beauty. We stopped and stared as they passed above us. There were six of them, young beautiful women dressed in flowing white garments and engaged in earnest conversation. If they were aware of our existence they gave no indication of it. Their faces were perfectly clear to us, and one woman, slightly older than the rest, was especially beautiful.

Her dark hair was pulled back in what today we would call a ponytail and although I cannot say it was bound at the back of her head, it appeared to be. She was talking intently to a younger spirit whose back was toward us and who looked up into the face of the woman who was talking. Neither Marion nor I could understand their words.

After the creatures passed by, Dr. Harlow asked his wife, "Marion, what did you see? Tell me exactly, in precise detail. And tell me what you heard." She reported her experience to be identical with his.

Beings from Another World
Aliens or Angels?

Although angels have gained new popularity in recent years, for most of us in the modern world, angelic sightings seem both unusual and doubtful. However, the ancient Celtic Christians took for granted that celestial visitors peopled their world. Ray Simpson, who helped establish the modern Community of Aidan and Hilda on Lindisfarne, notes, "In the Celtic as in the Orthodox understanding of life we are never alone, and God is never alone. God likes company . . . God has peopled the unseen world with the bodiless beings we know as angels."

Angelic visits are a common occurrence in stories of the Celtic saints. One of Saint Columba's miracles, for example, involved an angelic rescuer. The saint was copying scripture at Iona, when the monks around him noticed he suddenly looked startled. His fellows asked him why he was troubled, and Columba replied, "A brother at our monastery in Derry was working at the top of a large building there, and he slipped and fell. I ordered the angel of the Lord who was standing just here among you to go immediately and rescue our brother." The monks heard later that the man at their sister monastery had indeed fallen from a great height but was miraculously unhurt. When they reported this back to Columba, he explained, "How wonderful beyond words is the swift motion of an angel, it is swift as lightning. The heavenly spirit that flew from us when that man began to fall was there to support him in a twinkling of an eye before his body reached the ground. How wonderful that God gives us such help through his angels." Columba was apparently more impressed by the angel's speed than he was by its mere existence.

Columba was also far from intimidated by his angelic visitors. Another time, when he was asked to assist in selecting a new king for the throne of Dalriada (the Gaelic kingdom that at the time spanned the west coast of Ireland and the east coast of Scotland), Columba was firm in his mind about the candidate he supported. However, an angel appeared to the saint and commanded Columba to back a different man. Columba argued with the angel, and the heavenly messenger, infuriated, slapped the saint on his cheek. Though the angel appeared to the saint in a vision, the slap-mark was clearly visible for a long time to his companions. (Given the polarization of today's American government, it may be time for angels to get involved in politics again!)

Angelic assistance was not just for the luminaries of faith; Celtic Christ-followers believed that heaven's messengers protected ordinary believers as well. The *Carmina Gadelica* contains this prayer:

> *O angel of God who has charge of me*
> *From the dear Creator of mercy,*
> *Make 'round about me this night*
> *The shepherd's fold of the saints.*
>
> *Drive from me every temptation and danger,*
> *Surround me on the sea of unrighteousness,*
> *And in the narrows, crooks, and straits,*
> *Keep my small boat, keep it always.*
>
> *Be a bright flame before me,*
> *Be a guiding star above me,*
> *Be a smooth path below me,*
> *And be a kindly shepherd behind me,*
> *Today, tonight, and forever.*

The stories of the Bible that inspired Celtic faith are replete with angels. The opening chapters of Genesis include an angel in the Garden of Eden. Abraham, "the father of faith" for both Jews and Christians, dealt repeatedly with angel messengers. Jacob, who was the father of all the Israelite tribes, wrestled with an angel. Angels accompanied Jesus' birth and his entire ministry, and angels announced the highpoint of the biblical narrative—the resurrection of Christ—as well. The Hebrew scriptures contain 117 references to angels, and in the New Testament there are 182 references. Given that angels appear almost 300 times in the Bible, it would seem incongruous if heavenly beings did not have some involvement in earthly life in later ages.

When Celtic Christ-followers expected angels to be part of their experiences, they assumed that the biblical world and theirs were basically similar. Nowadays, the cultural setting of the Bible seems very different from our daily experiences; unlike the ancient Israelites, we drive cars and communicate at the speed of light. The Gaels, however, lived with wooden boats, hand-seeded farms, and communication from mouth to ear; they lived in practically the same way that Jesus and his companions lived. So they found it easy to imagine that the angels of the Bible inhabited their world as well.

Meanwhile, even if we modern believers accept that the shepherds heard an angelic chorus on the night of Christ's birth, we doubt that angels still sing in our modern skies. Angels are a New-Age fad; people who consider themselves rational disciples of the scientific method are less likely to be open-minded about angels.

However, opening our minds to the possibility of other-worldly beings need not contradict rational or scientific thinking—and these beings may turn out to be far more common than we think.

Over the past decades, many individuals have described to me supernatural experiences in which they saw what they assumed to be aliens, ghosts, gods or goddesses, or fairies. Their descriptions of these beings— shimmering, ethereal, frightening, powerful, beautiful men or women—resonate with the Bible's description of angels, but the reporters' predispositions may have caused them to label their sightings in other terms. People who are materialist or scientific in their thinking, for example, might be more likely to think in terms of "aliens," which are a bit more plausible to their frame of reference. Those who practice the Old Religion are apt to report what they see in terms of their pagan expecta- tions: a beautiful woman floating in the air is the Goddess; an invisible touch comes from the Sidhe (pronounced "shee," the faery-folk of Celtic myth). Exposure to shows like *Ghost Hunters* is likely to mean that any luminous or translucent beings are categorized as "ghosts." If, how- ever, everyone who claimed to have seen ghosts, aliens, fairies, and so on saw the world through the lens of Chris- tian tradition, they would likely label their experiences as angel sightings.

Although such sightings fall outside our normal expe- rience of the world, they need not contradict scientific understandings of our universe. If you have read any quantum physics, you'll know that the universe is, in fact, a decidedly odd sort of place, much odder than our "normal experience" might lead us to believe. C. S. Lewis, writing some forty years ago, stated: "To explain even an atom Schrodinger wants seven dimensions. . . . There may be Natures piled upon Natures, each supernatural to the one beneath it." Recently, Martin Rees, an English cosmologist and astrophysicist (and an Astronomer Royal since 1995 and Master of Trinity College, Cambridge, since 2004), commented, "All these multiverse ideas . . . lead to the extraordinary consequence that we may not be the deepest reality [and] . . . blurs the boundary between physics and idealist philosophy, between the natural and the supernatural."

The ancient Celts didn't have the same problems many of us do with accepting supernatural encounters; they assumed angelic intervention was a common factor in their lives. The growth of an oak from a tiny acorn, the fall of a shooting star, and the appearance of a shimmering, winged being—all were alike manifestations of the great and mysterious God.

While the Celts took for granted that angels hovered over the Earth, they also believed in demonic forces. Ancient traditions describing spiritual warfare exist outside Christianity as well. The earliest Taoists, for example, hermits who lived millennia before Christ, engaged in spiritual martial arts in order to free the world from the grip of demons' control. The Buddha, en route to his awakening, faced the temptations of Mara, the evil one. (Some Buddhists take this literally, others figuratively.)

Demonic conflict is a recurring theme in the life of Jesus recorded in the Gospels, and later New Testament writings make frequent mention of the devil and his cohorts. Anthony the Great, the Egyptian monk who was a model for many of the Christian Celts, focused his ministry on demonic warfare. The desert was the place of Jesus' temptation, and Anthony had similar experiences there.

His biographer and contemporary, Athanasius, chronicled Anthony's battle against evil forces. Anthony's first spiritual trial (described in chapter 5) was to descend into an ancient tomb, where the demons attacked him so ferociously that his body bore the marks of their violence. After triumphing in the tomb, he arose and began a new life of solitude in an abandoned desert fortress. Anthony did not allow visitors to enter this prayer refuge, but travelers outside "heard what sounded like clamoring mobs inside making noises, emitting pitiful sounds and crying out, 'Get away from what is ours!'" One group of travelers, hearing the noise, feared that thieves were attacking the saint, so they climbed up a ladder to peek over the wall. Inside, they saw no assailants—only Anthony battling invisible foes.

Today, modern psychiatrists would likely label Anthony as schizophrenic. It's possible modern psychiatry merely offers another vocabulary and mental paradigm for the same reality earlier generations described as demonic onslaughts—but if we dismiss Anthony's warfare as merely "all in his mind," we may overlook his and other ancient Christians' practical spirituality. They believed in the supernatural, but they were discerning as well: demons could cause mental distress as well as physical illnesses, they believed, but they also knew that many maladies came from natural causes. And Anthony was by no means unique in his battle against dark forces.

Cuthbert, the Celtic saint who evangelized the Saxons, was constantly engaged in spiritual battle. Once he was preaching to a Saxon crowd, urging them to follow Christ, when he sensed that "the ancient enemy, the devil, was present, come to hinder his work of salvation." He then addressed the crowd, urging them to beware of the devil, "for he has a thousand crafty ways of harming you." As he preached, an apparent fire broke out in the village, with smoke and flame seeming to spread from house to house. The crowd panicked and set about trying to douse the flames, but to no avail; water seemed to pass right through the fire. Cuthbert shouted that the fire was an illusion, a falsehood created by demons to distract the villagers from the gospel. He knelt and prayed fervently; the flames vanished, and the houses were as intact as they had been before the incident. Cuthbert then reminded his hearers that "the devil did not cease even for an hour in his warfare against man's salvation."

Cedd was a Saxon contemporary of Cuthbert who also battled supernatural evil. At the urging of King Ethelwald, he set out to found a monastery and chose a spot said to be accursed by an ancient act of dark magic; Cedd fasted and prayed there for the entire season of Lent. When Easter Sunday came, he pronounced that the place was cleansed, and he built the monastery of Lastingham there, thirty-five miles from York. The monastery bore good spiritual fruit through the centuries, and the chapel still serves a worshiping congregation today.

Fully a third of the recorded miracles of Saint Columba involve evil spirits. On one occasion, Columba was fasting alone on Iona, apart from his brethren. In a vision, he saw a wave of black creatures holding iron darts, attacking and striking down the monks of his monastery. Then, in his vision, Columba received a suit of armor from the Apostle Paul, like that described by the same apostle in the Book of Ephesians. Protected by the armor of God and armed with the Word of God, Columba spent the entire day in violent combat, taking on the demonic forces singlehandedly, a true warrior of the Spirit. When the exhausted saint returned to the monastery, he informed his fellows that they had been spared from the plague, due to his spiritual warfare on their behalf. However, he also informed them that the demon horde would descend upon a neighboring monastery. Columba warned the abbot of the nearby monastery, who immediately ordered the entire community to fast and pray against the attack. As a result of their prayers, only one monk died of the plague; the rest were spared because of their intercessions.

Warrior Spirits
Spiritual Battles

Ancient accounts connect demons and angels with martial prowess. The first angel to appear in scripture in Genesis carries a "flaming sword." In the Hebrew scripture (Daniel), the Archangel Michael appears as a warrior who fights demonic princes, and then shows up again in the Christian Bible (Revelation), where he wars against Satan and his angels.

Nowadays, images of angels swinging swords while dressed in Roman-style breastplates may seem rather archaic and fantastical. But we should take seriously the military imagery associated with angels and demons. Like the ancients, we live in dangerous times. While they feared the pillage of barbarian warriors and the onslaught of the plague, we worry about terrorist attacks, global warming, violent crime, and mysterious illnesses like AIDS and SARS. The specific forms of violence and death have changed, but the precariousness of life has not.

If indeed our realm is an intersection of visible and

invisible realities, then we can be grateful that our technological world still has room for angelic protection. When we're sick, we do well to listen to our doctors and use the latest advances in medicine—and at the same time, we can pray and invoke the aid of the heavenly hosts. (I see no reason why angels couldn't battle microbes as well as evil spirits!) When threatened with violence or accident, we take into account all we know of natural phenomena and human nature, yet we can still call upon heavenly resources for aid.

The angels are God's messengers. Hebrew and Greek words translated "angel" in the Bible are the same as the English word "messenger," and these words are used for both human and divine couriers. When we ask for angelic aid, we are simply calling upon God to send forth Divine servants (whether they be natural or supernatural). According to Evagrius of Pontus who lived among the desert ascetics, "If you pray truly, you will feel within yourself a great assurance, and the angels will be your companions. Know this, that as we pray, the holy angels encourage us and stand at our side, full of joy, and at the same time interceding on our behalf."

If you have an uncanny sense of unease, that's a particularly good time to ask God for angelic protection. If you become aware that someone far away is in need (as Columba did), you can ask God to instantly dispatch Divine servants to help that individual (even if she is on the other side of the world). When in peril or threat of any kind, pray for angelic protection, knowing that countless believers before you have done so. Angels are rarely seen, so we can never prove how much they have blessed us, but scripture and many witnesses attest to their powerful aid. The universe envisioned by the ancient Celtic Christ-followers was a friendly one, despite the forces of evil, a companionable spiritual world where humans were never expected to face hardship alone.

As for the demons, paying them too much attention is not healthy. In the preface to his book *The Screwtape Letters*, C. S. Lewis wrote, "There are two equal and opposite errors into which our race can fall about the devils. One is to disbelieve in their existence. The other is to believe, and to feel an excessive and unhealthy interest in them."

One man who avoided both extremes was psychiatrist M. Scott Peck, a famous author of self-help books. In his practice with mentally ill persons, Peck became convinced that the devil did in fact exist. In his book *People of the Lie*, Peck documented his observation of demonic deliverance ceremonies and concluded:

> Almost all the team members at both exorcisms were convinced they were at these times in the presence of something absolutely alien and inhuman. The end of each exorcism proper was signaled by the departure of this presence from the patient and the room.

Later, in *Glimpses of the Devil*, Peck noted, "The demonic is evil, and if we know nothing else about Satan, demons, or evil people, it is that they lie." He reaffirmed his observation that possessions and exorcisms were real, though uncommon, and added, "The diagnosis [of demon possession] is not one to be bandied about."

If you fear a demon behind every bush, you are en route to paranoia. And if you refer to demons often in your conversation, you're likely to frighten or alienate people needlessly, particularly if you ascribe all mental illness to demonic assaults. On the other hand, there are cases when supernatural evil is clearly indicated; in that case, you do yourself no service by ignoring reality.

The Catholic Church has a well-established tradition of dealing with evil spirits that requires four "symptoms" before a priest can perform a deliverance ritual: supernatural abilities, fierce hatred of holy things, supernatural knowledge, and the ability to speak in languages that the afflicted person has never learned. When these signs are present, supernatural affliction may be a reasonable diagnosis.

Demonic influences vary in variety and intensity. We may experience them as a heaviness in our emotions or as selfish thoughts that plague us. Distinguishing the subtle line between our own selfishness and demonic manipulation is often difficult, but in rare cases, evil spiritual forces do control individuals, at least to a degree. The term "possession" is not actually used in the Bible for this situation; the Greek word used in the scripture means literally "demonized." That biblical term is preferable, since "possession" wrongly implies ownership—and all of us truly belong only to God.

Demonization may be involved in cases where people seem controlled by invisible forces. These cases are frightening and potentially dangerous; you should only get involved if you are properly trained. The prerequisite training in cases like these is a regular habit of fasting and deep prayer. Even if you are a well-trained warrior of the Spirit, deliverance should never be attempted alone. We are always stronger and more balanced when we pray with at least one other person.

Movies like *The Exorcist* sensationalize demonic powers. The fear we feel in response may be a pleasurable thrill while we're watching the movie—but anything that exaggerates demonic powers is unhealthy. Remember, demons are liars! We have no reason to feel afraid of them, for Christ has overcome evil, and we can claim his victory.

If you feel afraid of supernatural evil, command it to leave: "By the name of Jesus Christ, the One who defeated you on the cross, I command you to depart from here and not return!" You may have to repeat the words several times, as Jesus did when he confronted Legion in the Gospels. These words are not spells you have to get exactly right for them to work—but words do have power to shape our own minds as well as the external world. Anthony and Columba drove demons away merely by making the sign of the cross, physically claiming the presence of Christ.

The ancient Celts came from a warrior background, and they were grateful for the "armor of God" Saint Paul listed in Ephesians 6. This armor is not something magic, like Harry Potter's invisibility cloak; instead, it is made up of the practical spiritual disciplines of truth, justice, peace, and faith. When we practice these, we are kept safe from demonic lies—and the only weapon we need is "the sword of the Spirit, which is the word of God."

As in most things, an ounce of prevention beats a pound of cure. In the past decade, I've personally dealt with a half-dozen cases where people were severely afflicted by demonic forces. In every instance, at a definite point the afflicted person had invited evil powers into his or her life. These individuals had practiced Satanism, Black Magic, or tribal witchcraft prior to the demonic affliction. Freedom from demonization came only after the individuals renounced their previous allegiance—in effect, told the evil spirits, "Get lost! I don't want anything more to do with you."

The ancient Celts had a custom they called "circling," a means of protection from all evil. The circle invoked God's defense in all directions, and it sanctified the circled space, acknowledging the power of the Divine Presence to protect. The practice of walking circles around an object or place was often performed on September 29, the feast of the Archangel Michael. The Celtic word for circle is *caim*, and Ray Simpson suggests, "To say the Caim or Circling prayer, stretch out your arm and index finger and turn sunwise calling for the Presence to encircle the person or thing you pray for."

We might walk around a home or property, praying God's protection as we go, or if we feel beset by spiritual attacks, we might draw a circle on the ground around ourselves, invoking the protection of God within that circle. The ancient Celts had specific "encircling prayers" like this one:

> *My Christ, my shield, my encircler,*
> *Each day, each night, each light, each dark*
> *My Christ, my Christ! My shield, my encircler,*
> *Each day, each night, each light, each dark,*
> *Be near me, uphold me, my treasure, my triumph,*
> *In my lying, in my standing, in my watching,*
> *in my sleeping,*
> *Jesus, Son of David, my strength everlasting!*
> *Jesus, Son of Mary, my helper, my encircler!*

Again, prayers and practices like these are not magical spells; they are means to increase our own inner faith even as we call for God's protection on the outer world.

Nevertheless, some people might regard circling as a superstition, especially as the custom pre-dated the coming of Christianity to the Celtic lands. But the druids' understanding of the protecting circle was a sound one.

The priests of the Old Religion said that evil cannot enter a circle, for this symbolic design has "no end, no break, and no entrance." With the coming of Christianity, the Celts learned that the circle represented the Almighty One. An early Christian theologian described the Holy Trinity as *perichoresis*, a Greek word that means "circle dance," and the circle of protection invokes the presence of the Trinity.

Ultimately, just as the best way to avoid a cold virus is exercise, vitamins, and a healthy diet, the safest way to avoid evil powers is to commit your life to God and practice the spiritual disciplines We have no need to worry about the forces of evil; Anthony, who knew more than most of us ever will about demonic attacks, wrote, "Wherever you are on earth . . . the Lord is near, do not be anxious about anything." And in the Christian scriptures, the Apostle James offers this good advice: "Submit yourselves, then, to God. Resist the devil, and he will flee from you. Come near to God and he will come near to you" (4:7–8).

When you walk in the light—the darkness simply isn't there!

I bind unto myself today
The power of God to hold and lead,
His eye to watch, His might to stay,
His ear to hearken to my need.
The wisdom of my God to teach,
His hand to guide, His shield to ward;
The word of God to give me speech,
His heavenly host to be my guard.

BEINGS OF LIGHT AND DARKNESS

Against the demon snares of sin,
The vice that gives temptation force,
The natural lusts that war within,
The hostile men that mar my course;
Or few or many, far or nigh,
In every place and in all hours,
Against their fierce hostility
I bind to me these holy powers.

Against all Satan's spells and wiles. . . .
Protect me, Christ, till Thy returning.
Christ be with me, Christ within me,
Christ behind me, Christ before me,
Christ beside me, Christ to win me,
Christ to comfort and restore me.
Christ beneath me, Christ above me,
Christ in quiet, Christ in danger,
Christ in hearts of all that love me,
Christ in mouth of friend and stranger.
I bind unto myself the Name,
The strong Name of the Trinity,
By invocation of the same,
The Three in One and One in Three.
By Whom all nature hath creation,
Eternal Father, Spirit, Word:
Praise to the Lord of my salvation,
Salvation is of Christ the Lord.
—Saint Patrick's Lorica
("Breastplate," as in Ephesians 6)

Despite their belief in the very real forces of evil, the ancient Celts saw Creation as a friendly place where angels and saints worked together with human beings to accomplish God's will on Earth.

11
CIRCLES OF STRENGTH
COMMUNITY

All streams flow into the sea,
yet the sea is never full.
To the place the streams come from,
there they return again.
—Ecclesiastes 1:7

We think of various bodies of water—creeks, rivers, ponds, springs, oceans—as separate entities. Yet in fact, all the waters in the world feed into each other in a never-ending stream. Molecules that now reside below the ground will eventually bubble to the surface, and then run downhill to form creeks or ponds. Creeks feed into larger rivers, which may in turn empty into lakes or oceans. We cannot build a wall around water; if we throw toxins into the tiny stream in our backyard, one way or another, that poison will eventually reach a larger body of water. On the other hand, the ocean's bounty will eventually become the rain that nourishes the soil, then rises to the surface and runs downhill, beginning the circle anew. Just as scientists view the blood that flows through our bodies as a single tissue, all water is interconnected.

We humans also share a common destiny: we are as interdependent on one another as the parts of the water cycle are intertwined. We cannot separate ourselves from one another, for our lives flow together in a constant current. Chief Seattle of the Nez Perce Tribe affirmed this when he said, "All things are connected, like the blood that runs in your family."

The ability to form relationships is one of the greatest gifts God has given humanity. By building friendships, villages, and societies, we water our civilizations; we make advances in technology, in the arts, and in spiritual growth. Of course, with great potential also comes great peril: as easily as we make friends, marry, and raise families, we can also hate, inflict injustice, and make war. Just as pollution spreads easily between bodies of water, so too can hatred and violence flow from human to human. In this sense, not all that much has changed since the days of the ancient Celts; the promise and the perils of our relationships continue to be one of the most important issues for happiness and survival in the twenty-first century. But the Celtic Christians give us wonderful examples of spiritual friendship, examples we can follow today.

Circles of Strength

For three long days, Kevin's sandaled feet had trod Ireland's cart paths and cow trails, through forests, up and down hills, and around lakes. His knees were sore, as he was no longer young, but the abbot pushed his body forward, hoping to reach his destination in time. The saint had once vowed never to ride a horse; he believed God intended his feet to be his sole means of travel. Days like this, though, he rued having made that vow. Time was of the essence, and the sun sped along its unrelenting course across the sky.

At last, as he strode along a dirt road beside the River Shannon, he sighted the top of the signal tower that overlooked Clonmacnoise Monastery. Almost there! He pushed his legs to a trot, despite their stiffness. As he passed a gap in the hedge beside the road, he could see the stone walls of the enclosure and the beehive huts within.

But where were the brothers? Normally a monastery would bustle with activity, but now the enclosure seemed deserted. He feared he was too late.

Kevin reached the wooden gate that guarded the monastery and made a gesture of blessing toward the porter. The brother bowed to the ground. "Greetings, Abbot Kevin, we are most honored by your presence. But—" He choked on his words.

"I am too late." Kevin finished the thought for him.

"I am sorry, Father. Blessed Bishop Kiernan went to meet our Savior the night before last."

Kevin sighed and steadied himself on his walking staff. He felt as if he'd been punched, all the air knocked out of him by this news, but years of training helped him to remain outwardly impassive. "God's will cannot be thwarted," he told the brother at the gate. "How did my friend pass away?"

The gatekeeper got to his feet but kept his head bowed respectfully. "Noon, three days ago, he appeared very weak and gaunt. He called us together and explained it was almost the time of his passing. He asked for—" The man paused.

The Abbot finished his sentence yet again. "He asked you to send a rider on a swift horse to Glendalough, so that I could come in time to see him." He sighed. "Your man rode well, and I departed as soon as that messenger arrived."

"Yes," the porter agreed. "Bishop Kiernan did that, and then he asked us to help him climb the tower for a last view of this settlement and the river. He loved this place very much."

Kevin nodded. "That was a good final gesture. Did he say anything after that?"

The monk nodded. "He asked us to lay him on a cot by the altar in the chapel. He told us, 'It is difficult for the soul to leave its mortal dwelling, even in the time of God's choosing,' and then he asked us to leave him alone. A few hours later, we saw a strange glow around the chapel, and we heard the sound of heavenly voices. Then we knew."

Kevin forced a smile. "The angels came to bear Kiernan's soul to the Throne."

CIRCLES OF STRENGTH

"Yes, holy Abbot. But, I am truly sorry. I know you were his anamchara—his soul friend. I prayed hard, till the moment of his death, that the two of you could be together again, before . . ."

"I prayed as well, brother, every step of my journey, but man proposes and God disposes. Now, can you take me to his body?"

Together, they went inside the ring-wall, past a stone high cross and piled rock huts, into the chapel at the heart of the monastery. There, several dozen monks faced the body that lay before the altar. They were chanting softly, but they parted as Abbot Kevin walked forward and knelt beside the body, and their voices fell silent.

Kevin looked at his friend's pale face. Kiernan had been little more than half Kevin's age, his head still full of curling yellow hair, his face unwrinkled. Why did God take home such a good servant at such a young age?

He touched Kiernan's cheek. "I'm sorry, lad," he whispered. "I'd give an arm or a leg to have ye back again, for just a short chat."

The cheek twitched.

Kevin jumped back.

And then . . . the dead man opened his eyes and slowly turned his head. "Kevin?" Kiernan whispered. "I knew you'd come see me."

Behind his back, Kevin heard the sound of astonished voices. The monks crowded in for a view.

"Bishop Kiernan," the foremost brother mumbled, "we thought for certain you were dead."

"My soul departed," the man on the cot replied. "The angels came to greet me, but . . . I told you . . . it's hard to leave the mortal shell. Besides," he smiled at Kevin, who was now weeping with joy. "I could not leave before enjoying one last talk with my dear companion. So I waited, hovering just below the eaves." He raised a quivering hand and put it on Kevin's arm. "I knew you would come. And now," he looked at his fellow monks, "we have already said our goodbyes, and I have only a short time. I wish to spend it in private counsel with my anamchara."

The monks reluctantly nodded and shuffled out of the chapel, buzzing with amazement at what they had just seen.

Abbot Kevin of Glendalough Monastery and Bishop Kiernan of Clonmacnoise were anamcharas—"soul friends," in the Gaelic language. Like David and Jonathan in the Hebrew Bible, they were two men bound by unbreakable cords of affection. The ancient Celtic Christians believed these soul friendships were necessary for normal spiritual growth. As Christ-followers, deep, rich relationships connected them to one another, and the Spirit flowed in a constant current between them.

Kinship
The Security of Relationships

Today, we have amazing ways to communicate and exchange information. The Internet allows easy communication across continents, and social networking enables individuals to connect with hundreds of online "friends." And yet, according to a 2009 *LA Times* article, "In 1985, when researchers asked a cross-section of Americans how many confidants they had, the most common response was three. When they asked again in 2004, the most common answer—from 25% of respondents—was zero, nil, nada."

And that is a real cause to be concerned for our society. According to University of Chicago neuroscientist John Cacioppo, "Just as the discomfort of scalded skin tells your brain to pull your hand away from boiling water, loneliness developed as a stimulus to get humans to pay more attention to the people around them and to reach out and touch someone." We really do need each other, and feelings of loneliness remind us of that fact. We are stunted—emotionally, spiritually, and even physically—if we do not connect with others in meaningful ways.

The ancient Celts obviously lacked the advantages of electronic communication, but they had something more tangible: multiple layers of relationships, providing strength on a variety of levels. Think of the Celtic relational world as a concentric set of circles: At the outside perimeter was the village, enclosed within the round walls of the circle fort. Within that were family homes, also rounded in shape. And at the heart of relational life was the anamchara relationship, two individuals with spiritually bonded hearts.

The first circle of relationship was the fortified village. If you travel to Ireland, Scotland, or Wales, you can see numerous examples of "ring forts." These are also called *cashels, raths,* or *dún* in Irish, or *caer* in Welsh, and they take the form of large circular embankments. These typically encompass a space 100 feet or more in diameter, and smaller circles of tumbled stone debris often lie within the circle. In Ireland alone, more than a thousand ring forts were originally constructed for protection from hostile humans and animals.

Patricia Calvert, an author who has written about Celtic history, describes the relational value of these physical structures: "When a farmer looked across the countryside, he saw raths belonging to his grandfather, father, and brothers. In a world of hostile forces—enemy tribes, hungry wolves, fierce weather—it was a comforting sight." Nowadays, you might not know the name of your neighbor two houses away from you—but ancient Celts would have known not only names but probably intimate gossip about all those who shared the rath with them. Loneliness was not an option, and with such close familiarity came the benefits of shared resources, physical protection, and emotional strength.

CIRCLES OF STRENGTH

For the ancient Celts—both pagan and Christian—circles were important spiritual concepts, as well as the shape of their physical dwellings. In incantation or in prayer, the caim (spiritual circle) was an important means of supernatural protection (see chapter 10 for more about this). The full moon was also a caim—a sacred circle endowed with spiritual protective power—as was the mightier blazing sun. In the Celts' minds, the circular rath that provided physical security would have had an obvious and natural connection with the symbolic circle of spiritual protection provided by magic or prayer.

And in all these cases, the circle itself was only a vessel for the real source of security: relationships with kin and kindred cosmic forces. These relationships were organized into a structure built from various roles.

If the rath created physical solidarity for the Celts, their chieftains were the ones who oversaw the entire network of relationships. Chieftains protected and expanded their holdings, through war, agriculture, or trade. Ancient stories paint pictures of idealized chieftains, people like Finn MacCool or Cuchulainn, individuals who were noted for their proud bearing, strength of arms, and generosity.

Druids served alongside the chieftains, giving leadership to society; their authority may have been even greater than their secular counterparts. Celtic historian T.W. Rolleston points out, "the druids . . . were the really sovereign power in Celtica." They were better educated than their peers; each druid had spent two decades of his life learning practical science, astronomy, and herb lore, along with multiple languages, in addition to ritual practices and divination. The druids kept the awesome power of literacy to themselves, thus promoting their people's dependency on their skills.

One of the great virtues of ancient Celtic societies was the full equality of women in a time when Greco-Roman cultures offered far less gender-parity. Celtic women arranged marriages and divorces, owned businesses, and inherited property. A wife could cancel her husband's business contracts if she deemed them foolish. In the ancient Irish epic titled *The Cattle Raid of Cooley*, Ailil, the king, is forced to compete with Queen Medb, his wife, in a contest of power. She demonstrates her superiority in both battle and sexual prowess, and then they vie at length to attain larger herds of cattle. In every realm—martial, sexual, and economic—Medb regards herself as the king's equal (or better). Likewise, women served in the druidic priesthood, with the same honor and authority as the male druids.

Within the protective circle of the rath, guarded by chieftain and druid, whether male or female, were the smaller circles of safety: the individual round houses, presided over by parents and grandparents. Ancient Celtic houses were always circular in shape, built either of stone or of timber covered with clay. They had tall, conical roofs of thatch, with a fire hole in the top. Perhaps the closest thing to an ancient Celtic home in the United States today would be a Navajo Hogan. The Hogan is octagonal, made of organic materials, has a chimney and stove in the very center, and most important, like the ancient Celtic round home, a Hogan represents the tribe's spiritual ideas of the universe: the six sacred directions, four sacred mountains, and the essential elements of earth, air, fire, and water. In a similar way, the Celtic home represented the cyclical nature of life, death, and rebirth, as well as the spatial arrangement of underworld and upper world connected by the beams of the world tree.

And like the Navajo Hogan, Celtic homes were built around the hearth. In Irish and Welsh tongues, the word "hearth" is derived from the word meaning "home" and "family"; the hearth was both physically and conceptually the "heart" of the home. As an old Irish proverb puts it, "The beginning and end of life is to draw closer to the fire." Fire was not only important for practical reasons, such as keeping warm, cooking food, heating water, drying things, and giving light, but it also represented a conduit for spiritual forces. In the Old Religion, the fire was an extension of the sun's power, and in Christian thinking, it represented the presence of God, who is "a consuming fire" (Hebrews 12:29). In Ireland, the hearth fire was traditionally extinguished and rekindled on Imbolc, February first, a day originally associated with the goddess Brigid, then later with the saint of same name. Sacred fires were also lit at Samhain time. Traditionally, Celtic wives cared for the hearth fire—and as they did so, they recited this prayer that tied the physical fire to the spiritual circle within which they lived:

> *I will raise the hearth-fire*
> *As Mary would.*
> *The encirclement of Brigid and of Mary*
> *On the fire, and on the floor,*
> *And on the household all.*
> *Who is that so near to me?*
> *The King of the sun, He himself it is.*
> *Who is that at the back of my head?*
> *The Son of Life without beginning, without time.*

Like the larger ring wall around the individual homes, each circle-house provided a sense of belonging and security, and it was likewise a spiritual circle of both human and supernatural relationships. Like God's self, the circle has no beginning and end. Like the world God created, the home was rooted in the earth, but its conical peak pointed to the heavens. Its enfolding walls were a womb of sorts, for this physical space saw the birth of each new generation into the family.

Many of us today would feel claustrophobic at the idea of living with our parents, children, and grandchildren in a single dwelling perhaps 25 feet in diameter. Ancient Celtic families, however, had no concept of privacy or personal space comparable to our expectations; instead, they had much more intense experiences of shared life, loyalty, and familiarity. Like all human beings, they had problems and conflicts—but loneliness was never an issue.

The circle of relationships extended beyond blood kin. Hospitality was an essential component of Celtic life, as this ancient prayer expresses:

> *O King of stars!*
> *Whether my house be dark or bright,*
> *Never shall it be closed against anyone,*
> *For Christ did open His house for me.*

> *If there be a guest in your house,*
> *And you share not with him,*
> *It is not only the guest who will do without*
> *But Jesus, Mary's Son, as well.*

Since the earliest times, the unwritten law of Celtic lands required hospitality to strangers. The Greek scholar Diodorus Siculus, writing a century before Christ, noted, "[The Celts] invite strangers to their banquets and only after the meal do they ask who they are, and of what they stand in need."

After the Gospel came to these lands, the Holy Trinity provided the Celtic Christ-followers with additional incentives for healthy relationships. Michael Mitton, a priest and teacher of Celtic spirituality, writes, "For them the Father, Son and Holy Spirit existed in perfect community, and therefore, the church needed to express this community life while it sought to serve the God who is Three." Ancient theologians thought of the Holy Trinity as *perichoresis*—the Divine Circle Dance—so God's very nature tied together sacred concepts previously contained in ring fort and round house. The New Testament Acts of the Apostles likewise affirmed the importance of Christian communal life:

> All the believers were together and had everything in common. Selling their possessions and goods, they gave to anyone as he had need. Every day they continued to meet together in the temple courts. They broke bread in their homes and ate together with glad and sincere hearts, praising God and enjoying the favor of all the people. (2:44)

With the coming of the Gospel to the Isles, many of the Iron Age ring forts converted into monasteries; we know this from contemporary historical accounts of cashels donated to monastic orders, and also from archaeological evidence. The transition from pre-Christian fortified villages to monastic communities probably proceeded very smoothly. Unlike later European monasteries, Celtic orders allowed "mixed" communities, with both male and female members, many of whom were married. Monasteries also included artisans, farmers, herders, and their families who worked on the community's holdings. Since they embraced all the classes of people common to the Celtic world, the "mixed" Celtic monasteries were little different externally from the communities that had once existed within the same circular walls. Their daily routines, however, were now based on a schedule of prayer and worship.

The monasteries gladly took on the duties of hospitality, serving as the hotels and restaurants of the Dark Ages. The monks and nuns strove to follow the Apostle Paul's admonition, "Welcome one another just as Christ has welcomed you" (Romans 15:7). Although monks practiced asceticism, sleeping on the hard ground and eating meager fare, they nonetheless provided their guests with comfortable lodging and full meals, including beer, vegetables, fowl, and fish.

As monastic settlements replaced the earlier ring forts, bishops, abbots, and abbesses replaced the chieftains of pre-Christian Celtic society. The heads of monasteries held sway over both spiritual and practical aspects of the new Christian communities; they were as much responsible for the planting of crops as for the seasons of prayer.

And like the chieftains of old, the new ecclesiastic heads of communities could be women or men, each individual being elevated to his or her position according to giftedness rather than gender. One reason for the swift and effective spread of Christian faith among the Celts was their empowerment of women. The Apostle Paul wrote to people of Celtic tribal background in his Epistle to the Galatians, stating, "There is no . . . male or female, for you are all one in Christ Jesus," teaching that would have reinforced their already-existing cultural beliefs. Christ's new followers in the British Isles would have been shocked if Patrick and other missionaries had urged them to put women in subservient roles; after a thousand years living in an egalitarian society, they were accustomed to full equality. Celtic leaders like Brigid and Hilda presided over monasteries with members of both sexes, and one ancient document claims Brigid was ordained to serve as a bishop (granting her equal status with Saint Patrick).

Although the basic shape of Christian communities followed that of older villages, from the role of women to the shape of the buildings, there was one obvious difference—the addition of high stone crosses. The Celts had lived for centuries under the shadows of standing stones; now they put their large-scale ambitions to work representing the victory beam of Christ (see chapter 4 for details of the importance of the cross for the Celts). Typically, the four directions bordering monastic communities were marked by four crosses, and these in turn were often named after the four Evangelists. These towering stone sculptures served to set apart sacred land from ordinary, and they also functioned as protective shields, guarding the holy circle from demonic forces.

As these Celtic followers of Christ adopted the ancient circles of relationships, setting ring forts and homes to their new Lord's service, they continued at the most personal level the druidic practice of the anamchara (soul friend). This concept is one of the most ancient aspects of Celtic theology. For the Celts, a soul friend was a spiritual guide, counselor, and private confessor; trust and accountability were the vital qualities of this relationship. With a soul friend, a person could obey the teaching of the Apostle James, "Confess your sins to one another and pray for each other that you may be healed" (5:16), and also follow the proverb "there is safety where there is much counsel" (Proverbs 11:4). In modern times, some Christians have a "prayer partner," and people in recovery programs such as Alcoholics Anonymous have a "sponsor" for accountability; the ancient Celt with a soul friend had a prayer partner, a sponsor, and an intimate friend all rolled into one. Even before Christianity, the Celts had the saying, "Anyone without a soul friend is like a body without a head."

Ultimately, the circles of relationship reached beyond even the boundaries of physical life. Death itself could not break the living current between kin. At the most ancient sites in the Isles, the dead were buried near astronomical sites and oak groves, so as to lend their powers to those still living. And at Samhain (our modern Halloween), the barriers between the realm of the blessed dead and the realm of the living came down, so that the deceased were believed to return and share in drinking and feasting with their living clansmen (similar to modern Day of the Dead celebrations in Mexico). The connections of clan and community were stronger than death. Following the ways of their ancestors, the Christian Celts also sensed that relational ties transcended the dread power of death. Walking in the footsteps of already-established Christian tradition, they sought the aid of their departed sisters and brothers who were now saints in heaven.

The Scots, Irish, and Welsh of the Dark and early Middle Ages lived in challenging times; food production, physical safety, and the threat of diseases were constant worries for them—but they found solace in their deep relationships. Each individual possessed multiple layers of camaraderie.

Today, we live in a vastly different age, where our relations are spread far and wide, rather than near and deep. Given the realities of modern life, how can we form circles of healthy and spiritual relationships?

Interflowing Lives
The Cost of Relationship

Ancient spiritual masters knew that nothing worthwhile comes without some form of sacrifice, and that is true of relationships as well. Healthy connection with others has a price. It requires that we let go of our pride.

"Pride" has many definitions, and I'm not speaking here of the healthy dignity each individual deserves to feel. The pride we must relinquish is the voice that tells us, "You're on your own. You'd be weak to ask for any help.

Doing so would be embarrassing. You'd lose face. People would think less of you." Barbra Streisand declared in an old song, "People, people who need people, are the luckiest people in the world," but very few of us want to admit when we need others.

A minister spoke on the topic of community at his church, and afterward, a college student from Africa, who happened to be visiting that morning, said to him, "What you said today would be obvious in the village where I come from. There, if someone has a canoe, and another villager needs to travel for supplies or medical care, they just go to the person with the canoe and ask, 'May I borrow your boat? I have a need.' But here in America, I see people all the time who would rather suffer than go next door and ask their neighbor to borrow something. It's crazy."

Many believers in America today lack community because they no longer attend those spiritual support groups we call churches. Their reasons may be fully justified: many churches have failed to be healthy communities, and congregations easily fall into hurtful patterns of closed-mindedness and control. As a result, many of us face a conundrum: while it is certainly true that churches have harmed people, we still need spiritual fellowship.

In his novel *The Screwtape Letters*, C. S. Lewis's master tempter, Screwtape, offers advice to a junior demon on discouraging Christ-followers from participating in churches. Screwtape urges the tempter-in-training,

"Make [the human subject's] mind flit between an expression like 'the body of Christ' and the actual faces in the next pew." He goes on to explain that the person in the next pew may be a great spiritual warrior inwardly, but humans can only see the superficial. "Provided that any of those neighbors sing out of tune, or have boots that squeak, or double chins, or odd clothes, the patient will quite easily believe that their religion must therefore be somehow ridiculous."

Finding a church that will water your spiritual life may be difficult, but it is not impossible. A flashy musical group or cushioned seats are not necessary; the pastor and congregation don't even need to agree with you theologically. Instead, look for folks that express their love of God by truly loving one another, and be open to the unexpected ways such a fellowship can nurture your soul. The ancient Celts were committed to communal living—but that certainly didn't mean they always agreed with each other! Sometimes, we need to be challenged by others' differences in order to grow.

The ancient practice of hospitality can also build friendships. We may not feel comfortable inviting total strangers into our homes the way the long-ago Celts would have—but what about the "strangers" with whom we rub shoulders every day? The folks who live next door or across the street, the people at work, the parents of your children's classmates? Reaching out past our comfort zones isn't easy, and there are plenty of genuine excuses readily at hand for avoiding hospitality. Our fast-paced lives, for example, may not give us time to keep our homes presentably clean or to cook a meal. But hospitality isn't about impressing people. It's simply about sharing food and friendliness—and we can do that as easily with take-out pizza as with a home-cooked meal; conversations can be equally meaningful around a restaurant table as in our own dining rooms. One couple I know sensed they needed more connection with others, so they reached out to six households they thought would enjoy getting to know one another, and then invited that group to a potluck-style meal. They repeated this process several months in a row, and to their delight, friendships sprouted out of these gatherings.

Another Celtic practice that seems especially fitting for our fast-paced world is the technique of creating community while "on the way." A good illustration of this is the ministry of Aidan, the Celtic monk assigned the task of evangelizing the Saxon kingdom of Northumbria. His job was a tall order: he had to communicate with people from a very different culture, in a second language, when they were predisposed to violence toward his kind. So first of all, Aidan refused to travel by horse; he believed that mounted travel discouraged communication. Instead, he resolved to wander on foot, so that he could converse with everyone who came his way. If he met a fellow Christian—whether Saxon or Celt—he would encourage that sister or brother, and say a short prayer for the person's needs. If he met a pagan of any tribe, he would give witness to Christ. In this manner, patiently and over many years, he built a large and effective network of relationships in the Kingdom of Northumbria.

In our hurry-up world, we are often so focused on our destinations that we forget the opportunities offered by the journey itself. Francis of Assisi, the spiritual child of the ancient Christian Celts, reflected this perspective when he wrote, "It is no use walking anywhere to preach unless we preach as we walk."

Today's would-be Aidans may need to forego cars. Walking is not always practical, but bicycling is an efficient means of travel, and one that allows opportunities to stop and chat with people much more easily than if we were to pull over in our autos every time we passed someone on the street. Likewise, public transportation allows for "chance encounters" (or Divine encounters) and conversation. Yes, most people on the subway or bus are reticent to open up to strangers, even to say hello; they're often afraid of each other. But the Spirit of Christ within us can produce an aura of humility and gentleness that breaks down barriers. We can learn to be sensitive to a gentle nudge from the Spirit to sense a need for healing or encouragement in the people we meet. Sometimes, even a smile can make a difference to the invisible spiritual community in which we live.

Finding ways to practice community is essential to a healthy spiritual life, and Celtic spirituality offers us plenty of examples to inspire us. The anamchara, however, may be both the most rewarding and the most challenging aspect of Celtic community. Many twenty-first-century people find a substitute for an anamchara in their professional counselor or psychologist, since a therapist is someone who provides a safe place to express confidences (what were formerly known as "confessions"). These professionals' services can be vital to good mental health, but bottled professional relationships fall short of the living water that soul friends share.

A counselor can be found in the local phone listings, but finding a soul friend is more art than science. You won't find "Anamchara" listed in the Yellow Pages, and you're unlikely to get good results posting a "soul friend wanted" ad on Craigslist. Your goal is to find a person you can thoroughly trust and whose opinion you respect, one who is wise in matters of the Spirit. Who is up to such a task? The ancients believed that God makes soul friends, and God is the One who must bring them together.

I have prayed very deliberately, "Lord, I need a close friend to pray and share life with, and to hold me accountable." On each occasion, God has led me to the friend I needed—and who needed me. A Buddhist proverb states, "When the student is ready, the teacher will appear," and I suspect the same is true of anamcharas. When our hearts are truly open to an anamchara friendship, we may even find that the individual is already in our lives. Soul friendships develop organically. They grow out of normal friendly interactions: hanging out, chatting at a coffee shop, sharing a few beers. They thrive when we are able to look past our differences and see the common heart we share.

Few of us living today in the twenty-first century have had the privilege to be born into the constant flow of a strong community the way the ancient Celts were—but we can build the circular currents of living relationships within our lives.

God did not create us to be lonely.

May Brigit give blessing
To . . . both man and woman;
Both wife and children;
Both young and old;
Both maiden and youth. . . .
Plenty of laughter,
Plenty of wealth,
Plenty of people,
Plenty of health,
Be always here.
—blessing from the Hebrides

An ancient Celtic community: circles within circles.

12
LIVING WORDS
SCRIPTURE

Whoever believes in me, as the Scripture has said,
streams of living water will flow from within him.
—Jesus (John 7:38)

Brother Fingal was in his cell, prostrated on a prayer rug, when the clanging bell interrupted his contemplation.

The brothers here at Kells in County Meath, Ireland, had already gathered for their morning prayers and then dispersed again for private devotions. It would be hours before the bell called them together for midday prayers. Something extraordinary must be happening.

The bell kept on ringing, and now he heard shouts. Fingal rose on stiff knees and stuck his head out the door. A farmer, the farmer's wife, and their two young daughters ran by; the monk recognized them as oblates of the monastery.

"Hurry!" the farmer shouted. "God forbid that they catch you!"

Fingal looked toward the monastery's watchtower, where he saw one of the monks swinging the alarm bell as he pointed to the east. Fingal's gaze followed the watchman's gesture. The old monk's breath caught in his throat.

A swarm of men crested a low hill outside the monastery wall. They were carrying shields, swords, spears, and axes, yelling in an unfamiliar tongue as they ran toward him. Vikings! He had heard of attacks on outlying monasteries and now—here they were.

"Brother Fingal!"

He turned toward the familiar voice of Abbot Dunstan, the leader of the monastery.

"Come with me, and gather others—to the chapel. We must guard our treasure."

Fingal reached back inside the door of his cell and grasped his staff. It was made of sturdy oak, but it was nowhere near as sharp or menacing as the weapons of the Vikings, who were now clambering over the monastery walls.

It would have to do.

Fingal caught up with Dunstan, and as the two sprinted toward the sanctuary, they gathered two more brothers: Liam, a stalwart older monk, and Kevin, who towered above the others and wielded a wicked-looking shillelagh. Kevin's presence encouraged Fingal.

The four hurried to the front entrance of the chapel and set their backs against the closed wooden door. Abbot Dunstan grasped his crosier in his fist. "Commit your souls to the Lord, my sons. Perhaps we will honor God with our martyrdom, or perhaps the Good Christ shall perform a miracle. Let us do what we can to save our dearest possession."

"Amen," the others agreed.

Fingal adjusted his footing and gripped the staff with both hands. "Lord have mercy," he murmured.

The Vikings were in the compound now, torching thatched roofs and putting God's flock to the sword. One of them, a stocky man wearing a gilded helmet, pointed toward the chapel and gestured. A half dozen of the Norse ran toward the four monks at the door. Liam ran to meet them, his fists clenched. A sword flashed, and Liam lay groaning on the ground.

Now Kevin leapt toward the foe, brandishing his club. One of the raiders went down. The next Norseman struck at the tall monk, but Kevin blocked the man's axe with his shillelagh and kicked the attacker's chest. Another Viking fell.

For a moment, Fingal wondered if they might be delivered after all, but his hopes were dashed as another of the raiders thrust his spear from behind—straight through Kevin's chest.

"Courage, my son," whispered the Abbot. And then the four remaining Vikings fell upon them. Fingal heard his own shouts as if someone else uttered them, and he saw his staff flying toward the attackers. Then, everything went black. . . .

His next realization was of throbbing pain, in his side and on the top of his head. He opened his eyes slowly and squinted up at the face of a brother monk staring down at him; it was Brother David, one of the novices of the monastery.

"Where am I?"

"In the dormitory. The Norsemen set fire to the roof, but we're patching it."

Fingal noticed other monks lying around him on straw and hide pallets. Apparently, the dormitory was now an infirmary.

"Abbot Dunstan—is he. . . ?"

"The Abbot has earned a martyr's crown," David replied softly.

Fingal sighed. "And our treasure?"

"Gone. The heathens took it."

"What did they want with it?" Fingal mused bitterly. "They don't speak our tongue—even the characters of their writing are different."

"Yes," David agreed. "Never were finer pearls cast before swine."

"For centuries, we guarded the Book of Colmcille. There will never be another like it. We have failed."

The other monk sighed. "I don't understand why God would let such a thing happen."

Three weeks later, Fingal's wounds were healing. Only a dozen of the brothers had died in the raid, and the survivors set to work restoring the Lord's cashel. While they were fortunate to still have their lives and their home, the monks nonetheless felt gloomy. Their abbot was dead—and they had lost their greatest treasure.

And then, on a rainy evening when the monks were gathered to eat, one of the oblates burst in. He dropped something on the table with a thud.

The brothers gasped.

Fingal put his hand to his heart.

The book! Its covers had been torn off—no doubt the Norsemen cared only for the gold and jewels that had encased the volume—but the pages were there, in all their illuminated glory.

"We could not defend it," Fingal exclaimed, "even with our blood, but God has preserved this holy treasure!"

The great treasure of the monastery—now known worldwide as the Book of Kells—is still safe today, carefully guarded and preserved on display at Trinity College Library in Dublin. Every year, thousands of visitors come from around the world to admire what a medieval scholar described as "the work, not of men, but of angels."

The Word of God
The People's Greatest Treasure

Ancient Celts treasured the ability to read and copy the sacred scriptures. Their reverence for literature led

Gaelic scribes to preserve all kinds of antique writings—
from the Greek philosophers to the myths of their fore-
fathers—but they prized the words of God more highly
than other texts. They viewed the scriptures as a stream
of wisdom, flowing from the Prophets and Apostles down
to their own age.

Historian Thomas Cahill writes, "Like the Jews before
them, the Irish enshrined literacy as their central religious act." Another historian, Leslie Hardinge, agrees
with Cahill:

> By far the most influential book in the development
> of the Celtic Church was the Bible. . . . It lay the
> foundation of the education of children and youth,
> and sparked the genius of poets and songwriters.
> It provided inspiration for the scribes . . . and
> affected the language of the common people,
> becoming the dynamic for the production of the
> most beautiful hand-written books ever made.

Celtic writers quoted the Bible incessantly. Saint Patrick
wrote only two short essays that still survive, but within
the modest scope of these two works, Patrick included
340 quotations from forty-six different books of the Bible!

Celtic scholars loved two books of the Bible especially.
The first was the Gospel of John; Erigena, the great Irish
theologian, said that this Gospel "touches the highest peaks
of theology and penetrates the secret spiritual heaven of

heavens, ascending beyond all history, ethics and physics."
The Celts also felt special attachment to the Psalms.

The Celts were a passionate people, and occasionally, their attachment to scripture could lead them to behave in decidedly unspiritual ways. According to legend, Colmcille (Columba), when he was a young monk living in Ireland, disputed the ownership of a handwritten psalter. He claimed the book as the property of his monastery, but another brotherhood also asserted their ownership. The result of that argument was a war between clans that claimed many lives. As a result, Colmcille was exiled from Ireland—and then apparently God took over, using Divine creativity to weave the threads of human flaws: Colmcille sailed to Iona, where he founded a monastery that would be a center for Christianity for centuries to come. That monastery, in turn, produced numerous scholars, scribes, and saints—and spread the light of Christ to the Picts.

Obviously, Celtic scholars of the Dark Ages loved the Bible—as ardently as any believers before or since—but the way they understood it differed from the way many Christians understand the Bible today.

Ancient Storytellers
Epic Tales with Spiritual Meaning

The pagan Celts and Saxons loved storytelling. Bards put ancient tales in poetic form, and rulers prized their skills. The flattery or contempt of a skilled composer was much like the power of today's media; it could raise or dash a chieftain's fortunes. The stories bards told of Cuchullain, Mabh, Arthur, and their ilk were more than just entertainment. These tales were mythic; they transmitted the core values of Celtic society.

No doubt, ancient audiences believed the epic stories were in some sense historic; that is, they thought the great heroes had actually existed. However, they also recognized that each bard individualized the tales, changing words and phrases to heighten the dramatic effect. In our world, television "docudramas" might be an analogy for the bard's tales. They are "documentaries" in the sense that we know something like this happened; as it says in the credits, "This story was based on real-life events." We also know, however, that screenwriters have adapted the facts to better fit an hour-long visual medium—and we don't believe that the people portrayed in these dramas looked as good as the television stars that portray them.

In Wales, I was privileged to spend a few hours with an older gentleman who delighted in telling me stories of Merlin and Nimue, Pwll and Rhiannon. He obviously loved having an audience, and he spun his tales with relish. His eye twinkled as he said, "At least that's as I tell it—and who's to say?" I could imagine a bard of ancient times using that same phrase.

When Christianity came to the Celtic lands, the stories of the Bible were added to the ancient tales; the old legends continued to be told, but the people gave Bible characters graver weight than the heroes of the Old Religion. The upshot was that Celtic believers in the early years of Christianity understood the Bible as primarily *stories* rather than as a source for theological beliefs. Abraham, David, Jesus, and Peter were new epic heroes.

Much later, during the "Age of Enlightenment" in Europe, Protestant ministers in Celtic lands emphasized the doctrinal nature of the Bible. Rather than a series of epic tales, it was a compendium of spiritual instruction and objective facts, based in history and provable by science, the absolute source for all Christian beliefs. This approach continues today in many Christian groups.

While many Christians still regard the Bible as a book of instructions or dogmas, others in the Western world are feeling the need for the meaning they find in grand epic tales. In the twentieth and twenty-first centuries, films such as *Star Wars*, *Avatar*, and *The Matrix* provide heroes that inspire viewers. Once again, imaginative stories are proving their power to shape lives and societies.

Returning to the ancient view of scripture as epic myths, powerful stories that offer us meaning and hope, would not mean we had relegated the Bible to the realm of fantasy. Because a story moves us doesn't deny that it happened in space and time. In religious studies, the term "myth" has nothing to do with the factuality of a story; we can talk about the "myth" of Dr. Martin Luther King Jr.'s March to Freedom, without denying that the Civil Rights Movement actually happened. "Myth" denotes the power of an account, without reference to its historical authenticity. In some cases, such as epic accounts of the struggle for equal rights, the stories would be weakened if we did not believe in their historicity.

Some of today's leading Bible scholars emphasize the value of again reading the scriptures as a set of mythic stories. John Goldingay, principal of St. John's Theological College in Nottingham, England, suggests we return to understanding the Bible as normative tales: "Stories are designed to work, to do something. . . . By portraying a past or imaginary or other world they issue a promise, a challenge, or an invitation that opens up a future or possible world." Reinhold Niebuhr, an important twentieth-century theologian, adds, "Myth is not history, it is truer than history." And when Huston Smith, noted scholar of comparative religion, says that symbolism is the most important language of religion, he means we need the deeper, larger-than-words imagery inherent in story to truly communicate spiritual truths that are too big for discourse and doctrine to contain.

Christ himself was a storyteller; he used parables instead of spelled-out doctrinal lectures to convey his deepest truths, knowing that stories are internalized far more easily than other kinds of communications. Stories stick with us; we recall them later in life, when they may open up to us with new meaning within the changing context of our lives.

In our world of technology, where so much of our reality is based on the scientific method, many of us may find we are hungry for tales of wonder and imagination, stories our hearts can access without applying the rules of observable, measureable cause-and-effect. When we read scripture from this perspective, our personal narratives become a chapter in God's larger tale, rivulets flowing into the great river of God's story.

Beyond Literalism
Reading the Bible Spiritually

The ancient Celts and their neighbors also interpreted the Bible in ways that differ from modern methods. They emphasized the importance of *spiritual meaning* over the literal meaning of the Bible. As Huston Smith explains, "Classical Christianity took it for granted that literalism could not do the full job, which is why 'Jesus spoke to them in parables.'" Likewise, the Apostle Paul contrasted the "letter that kills" with the "Spirit that gives life," and early Church Fathers such as Origen and Augustine were adamant that a merely literal reading of the Bible was inadequate.

Erigena repeatedly warned against interpreting the words of Scripture "only in their literal sense." He found that "the sacred texts themselves contain many contradictory statements," which must be interpreted in their spiritual-rather-than-literal sense "in the journey toward the truth about human and divine reality." For Erigena, reading the Bible "spiritually" was an exciting task, combining the human intellect, the contributions of Bible scholars, and the help of the Holy Spirit. He likened spiritual reading of the Bible to the thrill of piloting a ship through unknown waters.

Later Christians, however, were uneasy with such an approach to scripture, since it could easily lend itself to subjective interpretations that might lose the original authors' intended meanings. For example, an anonymous Saxon cleric who was rendering portions of the Hebrew Bible into his mother tongue in the early Middle Ages came to this phrase in Psalm 137—"O Daughter of Babylon, doomed to destruction, happy is he who repays you for what you have done to us, he who seizes your infants and dashes them against the rocks"—and made a significant change to the meaning. The Anglo-Saxon "translation" reads "happy is he who takes his own son and establishes him upon the Rock." In this "spiritualized" translation, a verse that apparently condones infanticide is turned to a much happier thought, that of raising one's child upon Christ, the Rock, despite the fact that such a meaning would have been alien to the ancient psalmist. As Paul Cavill, a professor of Saxon literature explains, "Thus the violence of even some parts of the Bible was modified and made more 'Christian,' perhaps because the translator knew his audience's tendencies well enough to know they needed moderating."

While we may be able to understand the temptation to "clean up" or edit the Bible in instances like Psalm 137, doing so damages the integrity of the historical document. Later generations of scholars insisted on facts-based Bible interpretation, and from there they went even further, eventually building the dogma that the Bible is without error of any sort—no contradictions, no historical or scientific fallacies. The more ancient approach to Bible reading was deemed dangerous inasmuch as the reader could make the text mean whatever she wished it to.

But as the pendulum of religious thinking swings back and forth, there is often a tendency to go to extremes. While correcting the errors of the past, we lose the treasures to be found there as well. We may find we could learn much from the ancient Celts' approach to scripture. The Word of God is living water—but have we bottled that water and packaged it, thereby losing some flavor? Perhaps we need to return to the old wells.

A college student in one of my world religions classes, who had just begun to read the Bible and was also taking a freshman composition course, paired these experiences and reached this conclusion: "The Bible seems to be in the genre of persuasive writing—the authors arrange facts so you will buy into their spiritual beliefs." Her comment echoes John's explanation for his Gospel: "These are written so that you may believe Jesus is the Son of God" (20:31). The Gospel writer is transparent about his persuasive intent.

Many Bible commentaries and sermons miss this persuasive aspect of the Bible stories. Instead of focusing on the plotlines, some religious scholars debate whether Samson could actually kill a thousand Philistines singlehandedly . . . or if archaeology can prove the fall of Jericho . . . or why the same incident is described differently by separate Gospel authors. Such investigations have value, but perhaps they also miss the point. If we ask, "What is the author trying to persuade me in telling this story?" we are reading more in the manner of the ancient Celts—and at the same time we are honoring the primary purpose of the text.

Reading for the author's persuasive intent can provide a more relevant understanding of the Bible than reading merely for historical or scientific factuality. Consider two differing approaches to the Book of Jonah. Many preachers have focused on the factuality of Jonah's journey in the belly of the great fish, but it's unlikely that this was the original author's main concern. Instead, imagine an ancient audience listening to a bard retelling the tale of Jonah. The storyteller looks at the children in his audience who are listening in rapt attention and asks, "What did you learn from that?" It would be a very literal child who responded, "Big fish can eat people." Instead, a thoughtful child might say, "You can't run away from what God wants you to do"—or, "God wants us to be nice to our enemies." These are good summaries of this Hebrew tale, deeper than its literal meaning.

As modern Bible readers, we have the benefit of a long perspective: we can view the entire winding river of Bible interpretation through the ages. Doing so, we see the advantages of interpreting the Scriptures as epic story and spiritual truths. At the same time, we are aware of the dangers of over-spiritualizing a text. With the advantages of hindsight, we can keep both extremes in balance, charting a middle course through the straits of Biblical interpretation. Quoting the Bishop of Durham, N. T. Wright, "We must be ferociously loyal to what has gone before and cheerfully open about what must come next." This combination of ferocious loyalty and cheerful open-mindedness combines both conservative and liberal outlooks into something new and living. Erigena also described this rare perspective, one that recognizes both the ever-changing context of our world and the never-changing nature of the Spirit: "The voice of the spiritual eagle strikes us. . . . May our outer senses grasp its transient sound and our inner spirit penetrate its enduring meanings."

The ancient Celts remind us that people in the past loved the Bible dearly—so much that they spent years copying it and were willing to give their lives to protect it—yet their understanding of Scripture differed from that of many contemporary believers. As we learn from them, we can allow scripture's rushing river to pour forth onto the parched landscape of our own time.

Read the Bible with an open heart. Let its stream flow through you.

> *Holy Scripture is a stream of running water,*
> *where alike the elephant may swim,*
> *and the lamb walk without losing its feet."*
> *—Saint Gregory the Great*

An initial capital from one of the Gospels in the Book of Kells reveals the loving intricacy and imagination the ancient Celts brought to their copies of the scriptures.

13

Gifts of the Imagination
The Arts

Then the angel showed me the river of the water of life,
as clear as crystal, flowing from the throne of God
. . . down the middle of the great street of the city.
—Revelation 22:1

On October 25, 2009, my wife and I sat in Pasadena's Rose Bowl Stadium with 96,000 fans, watching the Irish band U2 perform. To call the crowd "energized" would be an understatement!

Three-quarters of the way into the show, Bono, the lead singer, launched into a soulful singing of an older tune; in fact, it was several centuries older than the rest of evening's fare. The audience grew quiet, hanging on every word, as Bono poured his emotions into the old hymn, "Amazing Grace." As he held the notes of the verse, "that saved a wretch li-i-i-ke me," the crowd whistled and cheered. Then, as Bono exclaimed, "was blind but now I see," the band began their popular song "Where the Streets Have No Name," a passionate yearning for a renewed world. I was overcome by the beauty of the moment. The experience had risen above mere entertainment: thousands of people shared an act of worship.

Years earlier, in 1980, Bono and the Edge (the band's guitarist) had faced a crisis of faith. Fellow members of their Dublin church group confronted them, insisting that they could not follow Christ and play rock music. Bono and the Edge were conflicted: they wanted to do God's will, yet their souls yearned to sing. Fortunately for millions of fans, they prayed and concluded that they could serve the Lord—and still rock!

In the following decades, U2 has charted an uncommon course in the contemporary music scene: they have sold millions of recordings and retained a spiritual perspective. Songs such as "Gloria," "40," "Yahweh," and "Magnificent" incorporate sacred sentiments. U2 bridges the divide that formerly existed between "Christian" and "secular" commercial music, and by combining art and faith, they pay homage to their roots. Like their Celtic ancestors, the members of U2 weave spiritual faith into patterns of artistic excellence.

Music
A Divine Magic

For the ancient Celts, music was magical, a gift from the gods to humankind. One of the old stories concerns a great battle between the Fomorians (mortals) and the Tuatha De Danaan (the race of divine beings) that took place after the Fomorians captured the harp of Dagda (pronounced "dai," meaning the "Good God"). Dagda then strides into the enemy's banqueting hall, indifferent to a throng of Fomorian warriors. He begins to sing, and his harp springs from the wall, mowing down nine men in its path. The god grabs the harp and plucks its strings; the mortals begin to weep. He plays another set of notes, and the Fomorian host involuntarily burst into fits of laughter. Finally, he plays a slower tune, and the warriors fall fast asleep. Dagda then shoulders his instrument and walks out of the hall, stepping over the slumbering bodies of his enemies.

The story shows the divine power of the harp: it belongs to the Father of Gods, and possesses power to cause weeping, laughter, and blissful rest. Jewish scriptures contain similar stories of the harp's power. When a tormenting spirit seized King Saul, for instance, young David played his harp, and the evil spirit departed (1 Samuel 16:22). David is thought to be the author of much of the Book of Psalms, and his poetry repeatedly calls believers to worship with the harp.

This instrument was often carved on the great high crosses that dot the Irish landscape. The actual harps of ancient times were treasured objects expertly gilded and inlaid with precious stones, as befitted such holy instruments. The Brian Boru Harp, named after the Irish king who drove the Vikings out of Eire, graces Irish coins and is also the symbol for another national treasure—Guiness beer! Underlining the harp's importance, the tenth-century Laws of Wales mandate that "a man-of-rank must always keep his harp in tune."

Of course, the harp was not the only musical device the Celts enjoyed. One of the most venerated instruments was also the most ancient: the human voice. Bede, in his *Ecclesiastical History*, tells of a brother in the Abbey at Whitby who could compose songs such that "none could compare with him." The astonishing thing, according to Bede, is that this superlative minstrel received no formal training.

As young men often do, Caedmon joined his friends to party and have a good time. On such occasions, his companions would pass around a harp, urging each other to sing. Caedmon would leave the gatherings then, crestfallen, for he had a singular lack of musical talent.

On one such evening, he fled from a gathering and lay down in a barn. Out of the darkness, he heard a voice say, "Caedmon, sing me something!"

Startled, he replied, "I can't sing. That's why I left the feast and came here. I tell you, I cannot sing."

But the unseen caller demanded, "Sing!"—and to Caedmon's amazement, he opened his mouth and produced an exquisite song.

The next day, when Caedmon's peers heard his miraculous new talent, they brought him to Abbess Hilda at nearby Whitby Abbey. Hearing the young man's story, she instructed him in the Christian faith. He converted, joined the abbey, and gained renown as a troubadour for Christ.

As a convert from the Old Religion to the way of Christ, Caedmon illustrates the continuity of musical tradition between Celtic faiths. Like their ancestors, the early Christian Celts regarded musical arts as supernatural gifts—and intriguingly, God first endowed Caedmon with tuneful talent and subsequently led him to spiritual faith. The sequence of art preceding faith fits with the Celtic view that beauty and belief are equally sacred, both Divine gifts.

Ornamentation
Making All Things Beautiful

In the first century BCE, when the Greek historian Diodorus Siculus described the Celts, he was impressed by their skills in metallurgy and artistic adornment: "They wear bracelets on wrists and arms, and around their necks thick rings of solid gold, and they wear also fine finger rings." This description corroborates archaeologists' finds at La Tene in Switzerland, where Celtic graves from the centuries before the time of Christ yielded brooches, swords, and other intricately decorated artifacts. Likewise, the grave of a Celtic queen in Vix, France, dating from 480 BCE, contained a trove of golden utensils as exquisite as anything produced elsewhere in the world at that time.

Celtic metallurgy required great technical skill, and that skill was converted into beauty via the imagination of the ancient artists. Celtic jewelry is easily recognizable: swirls, curves, and abstract forms convolute into humans, animals, mythical beasts, and floral patterns. Celtic artists invoked the world around them—forests, lakes, mountains, stags, salmon, and fowl—and wove the beauty of nature into patterns of gold, silver, and precious stones.

An old Irish account suggests that the ancient Gaels regarded artistry in metal the same way they understood musical talent, as a gift from the gods. In one myth, the hero Cuchulainn appears to a craftsman named MacEndge, demanding that the artisan produce a shield with a unique magical design. MacEndge protests that he has no inspiration, but Cuchulainn threatens to kill the artist if he cannot produce a one-of-a-kind design by the warrior's next return. The craftsman trembles with fear, but an otherworldly being flies down through the smoke hole and promises his help. This god draws a design in the ashes, MacEndge copies it, and Cuchulainn is delighted with the resulting product.

These gifted craftspeople might be surprised, however, if they were transported into our time where they could see their work displayed as art, with no other function but to be admired. As Mara Freeman explains in her book *Kindling the Celtic Spirit*:

> In Celtic society there was no distinction between "fine" arts and crafts as there is today. The best art is found in the design and decoration of functional objects, from cups and bowls, combs and mirrors, to horse and chariot trappings and implements of war. Sometimes the most engaging pieces are found on the most utilitarian objects.

Like many indigenous peoples, the ancient Celts incorporated aesthetic beauty into their everyday lives. In the same way that they saw no boundary between the spiritual world and the everyday, they also saw no reason to separate beauty from practical usefulness.

When the Celts embraced Christianity, their craftsmanship continued to excel. They found affirmation for their work in the Bible, where the Hebrew scriptures laud "skilled workers" who can work "in gold and silver, bronze and iron, and in purple, crimson and blue yarn," and who are "experienced in the art of engraving" (2 Chronicles

2:7). In the early Christian era, the Celts created new forms of vibrant art—and produced works that still evoke awe today.

At the same time, Irish scribes wrote documents as visually beautiful as they were well composed; truly, the medium was the message. Before Christians intro-duced the Latin alphabet, druids had written documents in Ogham script. This form of writing consisted purely of straight lines, in intersecting vertical and horizontal directions. Such writing served well for chiseling on wood and stone surfaces, but was aesthetically limited. With the new faith came new mediums for communica-tion: curved letters, produced on dried skins with ink and quill. Celtic scribes introduced to Latin letters were exhil-arated by the new opportunities for artistic innovation.

Calligraphers ascribed their skills to supernatural aid. A scribe in Kildare was at work on a book, he claimed, when an angel appeared and showed him a special design, commanding him to produce the same image in his work. The monk protested that the skills needed for such work exceeded his capacity. The angel then commanded him to go straightway to Saint Brigid, his abbess, so she could pray for him to excel in the arts of illumination. He did so and subsequently created a splendid book, based on the angel's design.

Christian scribes took the simple geometrical shapes of letters and morphed them into the spirals, curves, and organic patterns of their ancient arts. If a scribe wanted to write the letter "c," he would not be contented with the simple half-circle you see typed on this page; instead, he added a spiral at the top of the letter, and extended the bottom of the letter into a meandering tendril. As a result, it was still discernible as a "c," but it took on a unique and playful persona. When this process is applied to entire books, the lettering alone is stunning.

The wide-ranging Celts also incorporated inspirations from their neighbors into written art. Saxon artisans were near at hand, and they, like their Celtic peers, were highly skilled in the arts. Saxon designs, more linear and geometric than those of the Celts, provided balance and counterpoint for the Gaels. From further afield, the artistic designs of the Egyptian Coptic Christians—bright colors, geometric knotwork, and semi-natural human forms—found their way into the manuscripts produced by Irish and Scottish monks.

With these combined influences, Celtic calligraphy went beyond the imaginative shapes of letters and words; scripts became frameworks to support drawings, knotwork, and illuminations. Ancient manuscripts like the Book of Kells and the Lindisfarne Gospels still evoke admiration and draw visitors from around the world to gape at their beauty today. A scholar of the last century, describing a page in the Book of Armagh, wrote:

> In a space of about a quarter of an inch . . . I counted
> with a magnifying glass no less than one hundred

and fifty-eight interlacements of a slender ribbon
pattern. . . . No wonder that tradition should allege
that these unerring lines should have been traced
by angels.

Unfortunately, written texts are perishable, and much
of the brilliance produced by Gaelic scribes has been lost
over time. However, their peers also produced inspiring
works of a more durable nature: stonework. Their most
amazing sculptures are the high crosses that still stand
proudly in England, Scotland, and Wales. Archaeologist
Hilary Richardson notes:

> Irish high crosses are unique documents in the
> history of sculpture. Carved at a time in Western
> Europe when there was little opportunity either
> to commission or produce work of a monumental
> character, they stand unrivalled in stone in the
> grandeur of their conception and executions. . . .
> The Crosses of Ireland and Britain are practically
> the only elaborate freestanding monuments of the
> early Middle Ages.

While calligraphy expressed Celtic artistic skill on a
small scale, the high crosses display the Gaelic genius
on a scope no one can miss. Twice—or thrice—human
height, ancient stone crosses still loom over the borders
of now-ruined monasteries, mark the graves of long-ago
saints in ancient graveyards, and declare their praise in

the centers of towns and villages. Celtic sculptors chiseled knotwork, geometric patterns, spirals, and human forms from top to bottom of these cruciform monoliths.

In doing so, they brought skills first developed in prehistory into the service of the church. Ireland, Scotland, and Wales are peppered with prehistoric stone monuments—standing stone circles, dolmens, and passage tombs all attest to an ancient genius for engineering with stone. These primordial skills wedded well with the new faith. Biblical stories—Jacob wrestling with the angel, Daniel in the lion's den, David playing his harp, and, of course, Christ on the cross—were framed amid the forms of the pagan Celtic past. Combining the best aesthetic traditions of the Celts over thousands of years, the high crosses display the adaptive and artistic genius of their makers.

The Christian Celts also produced architectural monuments noteworthy for their time. These may seem unimpressive when compared with the scale of later cathedrals and castles, but Celtic masons made buildings that were the peak of architectural sophistication in their time. Throughout Ireland, more than seventy round towers remain today. Originally, these marked the locations of monasteries, though in many cases the monastic structures surrounding the towers have fallen into ruin and nearly disappeared. The fact that these towers—some over a hundred feet tall—still remain is a tribute to their builders' skills.

They all follow a similar shape and set of proportions: tall thin cylinders topped with steep cones. Although they first appeared in the Christian era, these examples of Celtic building are—like the high crosses—a continuation of earlier pagan arts. Iron-Age Celts built *brochs*, round towers of stones fitted without mortar that were the most sophisticated efforts of their time. Monastic round towers were built upon the same foundational principles, but added adhesive materials so that they could exceed the height of their predecessors.

Curiously, no one today is certain what purpose the Irish round towers served. Were they lookout towers, belfries, strongholds to protect monastery treasures? These are only historians' conjectures; in all their copious writing, none of the ancient monks or nuns described the function of their towers. Perhaps Dark-Age masons erected these soaring monuments for the same simple reason that their peers hunched over delicate illuminated parchments, while others patiently chiseled stone crosses: something inside them drove them to produce things of beauty. For the ancient Celts, any artistic undertaking—whether a song or a lettered page, a stone monument or a building—was an expression of God's glory revealed to the world.

Re-Imagining the World
Art and the Spiritual Life

The legacy of Celtic Christian artists calls us to bring the splendor of God's beauty into a society where so many things are quickly, mechanically, and soullessly made.

GIFTS OF THE IMAGINATION

They challenge us to use the power of our imagination. In the modern world, however, imagination has often been relegated to children, as though it were something we should outgrow as we develop our full, rational faculties.

C. S. Lewis, who knew that imagination has a far greater role to play in our understanding of the world, once remarked, "Reason is the natural order of truth; but imagination is the organ of meaning." Imagination harnesses our minds to seek out things that are greater than our rational minds can conceive—and such things do exist; they are not mere make-believe. Imagination allows us to glimpse realities we can't yet perceive with our five senses. Without it, we humans would never have ventured past what we could see in the here-and-now, and we would still be living in caves, hunting and gathering.

Our imaginations prove we are truly made in the image of the Divine Creator. From the first centuries of Christian faith through to the Renaissance, believers understood that artists played a crucial role in God's Kingdom on Earth. Artists had the vital job of producing images of invisible realms, creating "thin places" where a song, a painting, or a statue allowed mundane and sacred realities to intersect.

Unfortunately, later expressions of the Christian faith sought to undo the world-affirming influence of the ancient Celts and their neighbors. In recent centuries, "Christian" art was divorced from daily, functional objects. Spiritual music was limited to hymns and organ compositions produced for performance in church gatherings; religious fine art was made only for stained-glass windows in church buildings; and "sacred" architecture developed in lines deliberately set apart from the style of other public buildings. With this great divide, over the centuries came a lowering of the standards for "Christian art." Since it did not have to compete with the world's great "secular" artists, it often settled for trite and sentimental expressions of the faith. As much of Protestant Christianity, in particular, focused on evangelism as the primary goal of the Christian life, Christian art became a propaganda tool rather than an expression of a deep and powerful perception of reality. In the process, Christian art became even more watered down artistically. No wonder that the twenty-first century hears so many voices claiming that Christianity is irrelevant!

At the same time, a growing movement among Christians celebrates art—and not just for the sake of evangelism. Increasingly, artists who are believers focus on making good art, rather than on making explicitly "Christian" art. C. S. Lewis expressed the motto of this new movement when he said he believed in God, "Not because I can see him, but by him I can see everything else." Likewise, songwriter and producer T. Bone Burnett told the *L.A. Weekly*, "If Jesus is the light of the world, there are two kinds of songs you can write. You can write songs about the light, or you can write songs about what you can see from the light. That's what I try to do." Put another way, artists increasingly recognize that their work is not necessary to convince the world regarding God, but their efforts are necessary simply because God has made them to be artists; creating art is their Divine calling, the way they live out God's presence within their beings. Artists create culture, working as the point at the end of God's pen—and some culture-makers recognize that reality.

You may be thinking, "This is fine for artists, who are a small and elite group of people, far distant from my own hard-working, bill-paying, laundry-washing world." But the ancient Celts affirmed that we are *all* artists of one sort or another. The Celtic way is to knot things together: the sacred and secular, art and ordinary life. If we heed the distant call from the Celts' ancient world, we will begin to re-tie the sacred knot in our lives.

God made you in God's image; God is the Creator; and so you too are a creator of one sort or another. Whatever talents you have—and you have many potential talents you have forgotten or not yet developed—reflect the Maker who dwells inside you. Your imagination may be asleep, but it is ready to wake up. Like Caedmon, you may protest, "I cannot sing"—but surely you find your foot tapping out tunes on occasion. "I'm not an artist," you say—but do you find yourself doodling in the margins of your paper, spontaneously producing designs? And granted, you are probably not an architect—but I'll bet you like to paint walls or at least pleasingly arrange the furniture and pictures in your home. You do these things because of the One in whom you live and move and have your being (Acts 17:28). Sewing, gardening, woodworking, playing the guitar, dancing, writing, even seemingly ordinary problem solving: all are ways that God expresses Divine creativity through you.

God is delighted when you become the person you were made to be. You may deny, disregard, or hide your talents because "I'm not a professional" or "I'm not really good at this." Stop listening to the critics around you, and most important, silence that brutal critic who lives inside your own head. The All-Maker made you in the Divine image and calls you to express the sacred creativity that lies within you. Your gifts are from God no less than the songs of Caedmon or the lettering of the Kells scribes; they may not be as highly developed, but they come from the same Source and fulfill the same purpose: to reveal God's presence in the everyday world.

As children, many of us enjoyed creative activity that has since been buried and forgotten. I have a friend who won an art contest in elementary school, and many years later, while unemployed, he decided to take up paint and brush again. To everyone's delight and astonishment, he turned out to be a painter of unusual talent who won awards and displayed his art in noted exhibitions. His talents had lain dormant for many years, but they were always there in nascent form.

What gifts of yours lie buried? It doesn't matter whether you turn out to be a Picasso, a Bono, or someone

GIFTS OF THE IMAGINATION

who paints for your own pleasure or sings in the shower. Let your gift of imagination flow. By unleashing your God-given artistic self, you draw closer to God—and the world draws closer to God's design, because you express the *Imago Dei*.

So take that sculpture class you've always wanted to enroll in . . . buy a penny whistle or a harmonica and practice . . . write haikus . . . plant flowers . . . audition for a part at a community theater . . . take dance lessons and whirl your partner. Shatter the dams that hold back the river of your imagination. Your gifts are part of the Divine mosaic, a color in God's vast box of crayons.

Join the flow of Creation. Start coloring!

The world will pass away,
but love and music last forever.
—Gaelic proverb

Ancient High Crosses reveal the Celts' creative skills.

14

Christ in Neighbor and Stranger
Hospitality

I was thirsty and you gave me something to drink. . . .
I tell you the truth, whatever you did
for one of the least of these brothers of mine,
you did for me.
—Jesus (Matthew 25:35, 40)

Curls of long blond hair whipped across the young woman's face as she squinted against the spitting rain, looking out at the hills of Leinster. Mists swirled around the chariot, and dark skies brooded overhead, mirroring the darkness she felt inside her soul.

"Don't scowl so, Brigid." The gravelly voice of her father, Dubthach, rumbled beside her as he handled the horses' reins. "You could do worse than serve as bond woman for King Dunlaing. Perhaps you'll bear him sons. Besides, you ruined all your chances of wedding as a free woman, so this is what you get." He leaned over the side of the chariot and spit. "Some Ris favor their slaves over their law-wives. It's not so bad."

"I am already wed to a king," she replied in a bitter whisper.

"What's that, lass? Can't hear you."

"I am the bride of Heaven's High King."

"Ptah!" His shoulders shook so hard with his laughter that the chariot lurched. "I wish that madman Padraig had never set foot in my cashel. Filled your head—and your mother's—with crazy ideas."

Brigid frowned. Sometimes, it was hard to believe this man was really her father. Her mother, Brocca, was of an altogether different nature; she had a soft voice and warm eyes that saw through to the soul. Brocca's union with the coarse chieftain had come about because she was his slave. And after today . . . Brigid would also belong to a man.

She choked back the bile that rose in her throat, gripped the chariot rail with a shaky hand, and tried to breathe. *Sweet Lord Christ*, she prayed silently, *I am yours—yours alone. I love you as I shall never love mortal man. Sweet Jesus, have mercy. Christ have mercy.*

Brigid and her father leaned forward to steady themselves as the chariot bumped up the side of a steep hill. They rose above the mists, and the drizzle ceased. Ahead, Brigid saw a wooden stockade and smoke rising from a dozen round thatched roofs.

Dubthach nodded approvingly. "Not such a bad place to live, eh?"

"Ho there! Welcome." A stooped man, his dark face battle-scarred, arms covered with golden torcs, emerged from the stockade's entrance.

"Bow, girl." Dubthach shoved Brigid into a subservient position.

She glanced up at the swarthy man. Was he the king? Now she dreaded her fate even more.

"This the wench? I'm surprised you'd sell your own daughter."

Dubthach shrugged. "I have many daughters—and also sons. I cannot feed them all, so—I choose to share my wealth with my friends." He bowed slightly.

The king walked over to the side of the chariot, reached over the railing, and pulled up Brigid's chin, scrutinizing her face. She winced.

"She's not bad," King Dunlaing muttered.

Dubthach smiled ingratiatingly; he was liege-bound to Leinster. "She's a fine healthy girl, and you'll be well pleased. Come, let us settle on the fee." He stepped down from the chariot.

Brigid started to follow him, but Dubthach stopped her with a gesture. "You stay here."

She could hear the two men speaking as Dubthach hitched the horses. "This daughter of mine is worth at least a dozen cows, I would say."

"I was thinking perhaps a new fine mail-coat?" the king replied.

"How fine?"

"No sword made could go through the links. And perhaps you'd like a wolf-hound to go with that?"

Their voices faded as the two men disappeared into the stockade, and the forlorn girl lifted her gaze to the sun now emerging between parted clouds. *Bright heaven's Sun, O my Radiant One—what am I to do? My own father would barter me for armor and a dog . . . but I am smitten with love for you. I would gladly slit my own throat rather than submit to these beasts, but you forbid that. Save me, my precious Love. I only want you.*

"'Scuse me, girl."

She whirled about to face the speaker, a stoop-shouldered man, missing half his teeth, clad in a pile of moldy rags that stank even two arm's-lengths away.

"I—I haven't had a decent meal for days," the man said. "Just roots from the ground, no strength in 'em. I'm an honest man, miss. I swear it by Lugh. Just fell on hard times, I did. Would you happen to have a few coins to spare? I'm wastin' away, I am."

She whispered to herself, "Hidden within you is my Lord, disguised as the 'least of these.'"

"Eh, what's that you say, girl?"

"I was recalling the words of God's Son," she replied. "I'll help you if I can." Her eyes darted around the chariot for something of value. They lit upon—

Her father's sword. It was an heirloom deemed magical by virtue of druids' spells, and the jewels on its gilded pummel glinted in the sun. She grasped it by the scabbard and then handed it over the chariot rail. "Take this, my good man. Sell it and you can feed yourself for months—maybe a year even."

The beggar's eyes widened as though they would pop out of his head. He stammered, grasped the weapon with both hands, and then scampered quick as a hare over a nearby hedge and out of sight.

"Well now, it's all settled!" Dubthach and the king reappeared, her father's arm over the king's shoulder. "I'm a richer man, and His Highness has a right fine golden-haired maid. She'll bring you happiness, I'm sure your . . ." His voice trailed off. "Where's my sword?"

Brigid bit her lip. "There was a homeless man. He needed it."

"*What?*"

"He looked like a dirty beggar—but it was really my Lord Jesus, who said 'Whatever you do unto the least of these, my brothers, the hungry, and naked—'"

"Where's my sword?" Dubthach shouted.

"Surely, Father, you'd rather provide food for a poor unfortunate man, than hoard that old piece of steel?"

Her father replied with an oath, but he was cut short by a word from the king.

"Dubthach, you didn't tell me this girl is touched in the head."

Dubthach scowled uneasily.

"The deal's off. I'll not have a crazy woman in my house."

The king gave a bark of laughter. "This wench might give away everything I own." He strode back inside his stockade.

Dubthach glared at his daughter, pulled back a hand to strike, and then dropped it with a sigh. "Very well," he muttered. "But don't think I'm going to keep you under roof for long. There's no one'll have you even for a servant girl nor take you for wife as long as you're doing mad things like this. Soon now you'll have to find your own way in life." He untied the horses from their post and climbed back in the chariot.

Brigid ducked her head to hide her grin.

This story is adapted from *The Life of Brigid* contained in the Book of Lismore, a medieval Irish manuscript. Accounts of Brigid's deeds always emphasize her love for Christ and her avid devotion to those in need. As a child, she was constantly passing on her possessions to the poor, and as an adult, she founded a monastery that was said to have fed every needy person who ever came there. Sean O'Duinn, a monk of Glenstall Abbey and lecturer on Celtic spirituality at the University of Limerick, says, "She stands unchallenged as the supreme example of charity to those in need."

Brigid's concerns went beyond mere charity; she also used her considerable influence to bring forth justice in Ireland, championing causes such as women's rights, protection for orphans, and advancement of education. As the story in chapter 3 also reveals, in a world where women had very few options, Brigid insisted on choosing her own way. She refused to become the property of any man. Instead, she lived out the call of the Prophet Amos: "Let justice roll on like a river, righteousness like a never-failing stream!"

The power of Brigid's life can be seen by her influence five centuries later. In his autobiography titled *Urban Iona*, pastor Kurt Neilson tells how Brigid touched his life in the twenty-first century when his wife was in labor with their third child and complications arose. An ancient Irish prayer came to his lips: "Come Brigid, come foster mother of Christ. Come to the bedside of this your daughter. Come with strong hand and healing touch, in the name of the One who is three." As the situation became desperate, he prayed again, "If you want to be part of the ministry of the parish, and of mine, and if you want us to take better care of the poor and lost on the street outside the church doors, then I'll see to it. Only save my child, save my wife." The baby's vital signs steadied, and an hour later she was born healthy.

Pastor Neilson remembered his promise. Shortly after that, the church's Wednesday night food ministry was named "Brigid's Table." The church set an icon of Brigid in the dining hall that portrayed the saint holding a scroll with the words "to save every miserable man." Later, Neilson's church began a ministry of hospitality to the prostitutes who worked in the urban neighborhood where it was located. This program is called "Rahab's Sisters" after the hospitable prostitute in the book of Joshua. Each week, women from the parish go out into the streets and befriend sex workers outside, inviting them into a secure space for food, warmth, supplies, clothing, referrals, prayers if requested, and—above all—unconditional hospitality. Neilson reflects on these ministries of his parish by quoting an old Irish poem: "Often, often goes the Christ in the stranger's guise."

Jesus' longest parable, contained in the twenty-fifth chapter of the Gospel of Matthew, has inspired Saint Brigid, Kurt Neilson, and countless others to serve others. The parable recounts how, at the final Judgment, the King "will separate the people one from another as a shepherd separates the sheep from the goats." Curiously, both the group that Christ rewards and the group he sends away seem surprised. They are not judged by their nationality, nor by their occupations, nor even by their religious beliefs.

Christ tells the righteous, "Come, you who are blessed . . . take your inheritance. . . . For I was hungry and you gave me something to eat, I was thirsty and you gave me something to drink, I was a stranger and you invited me in, I needed clothes and you clothed me, I was sick and you looked after me, I was in prison and you came to visit me."

The righteous reply, "When did we do those things?"

And Jesus tells them, "I tell you the truth, whatever you did for one of the least of these brothers and sisters of mine, you did for me."

Centuries later, Christians created various litmus tests for salvation—ways to distinguish those within the Kingdom from outsiders. These tests included baptism, confirmation, and confession in some churches, and responding to an "altar call" in others, saying a "sinner's prayer," or following the "Five Steps to Salvation." Few modern churches mention Jesus' own standard for defining the "sheep" and the "goats": whether or not one cares for others in need. And while churches emphasize the presence of Christ in sacred buildings, in rituals, or in praise songs, they sometimes forget where Jesus himself promised to reside—in people who are hungry, thirsty, and poor.

The Celtic Christians kept sight of Jesus' very practical and earthly instructions for ministry. Pelagius—the first Celtic theologian, in the fourth century—set the tone for his brothers and sisters in the years to come. He wrote:

> There are some who call themselves Christian, and who attend worship regularly, yet perform no Christian actions in their daily lives. There are others who do not call themselves Christian, and who never attend worship, yet perform many Christian actions in their daily lives. Which of these two groups are the better disciples of Christ?"

He goes on to affirm that those in the latter group are truly Christ's disciples, saying, "If a person can walk that way without ever knowing the earthly Jesus, then we may say that he is following the spirit of Christ in his heart." As to what constitutes a Christ-like life, Pelagius explains, "A person who has heard that God commands people to be generous, and then shares what he has with the poor, is truly wise." The Roman clergy of his day eventually convicted Pelagius of heresy. Nonetheless, his insistence on a pattern of Christ-like compassion remained throughout the Dark Ages in the Celtic churches.

And in the twentieth-century, the ancient Celtic spirit continued to inspire Christ-followers. George MacLeod, who was descended from a long line of Presbyterian ministers in the Hebrides, chose to serve a church in Glasgow during the Great Depression of the 1930s. MacLeod needed a way to provide hope—and jobs—to unemployed Scottish workers, so he transported groups of impoverished laborers to the Isle of Iona, where Columba's ancient abbey lay in ruins. They rebuilt the ancient church building and established a renewed Iona Community that embraced Columba's passion for faith-in-action. Today, the re-established Iona Community continues to work for justice and peace in Christ's name. Like St. Brigid before him, George MacLeod was inspired by Jesus' promise: "Whatever you did for one of the least of these brothers and sisters of mine, you did for me."

MacLeod wrote:

Inapprehensible we know you, Christ beside us.
With earthly eyes we see men and women,

exuberant or dull, tall or small.
But with the eyes of faith,
we know you dwell in each.
You are imprisoned in the . . . dope fiend and the drunk,
dark in the dungeon, but there you are.

Jesus' promise that he would be present in needy neighbors impelled his Gaelic followers to service, and another belief also moved them to action—their faith in God's ability to provide whatever they needed for these tasks. Often, people long to help others but fear stops them. "I'd like to give, but I have too little for my own needs." The Celtic saints' faith overcame such thoughts.

Brigid and Columba provide examples of God's provision. Ancient traditions pair Brigid with her specially blessed cow, a wondrous animal that not only supplied milk for the saint but also brought forth "rivers and lakes" of milk so that she always had super-abundance for the poor and needy. Likewise, Columba once watched a poor man named Nesan, who possessed a herd of only five cows, give from his small herd to provide hospitality for a poor stranger. Columba then promised Nesan that God would reward his generosity by increasing the herd to one hundred and five—and it happened just as Columba promised.

Sometimes, though, we don't worry so much about our lack of material goods as we do about our shortage of time and energy. The old priest in Yeats' poem "The

Ballad of Father Gilligan" has this problem; he is already exhausted from a long day of service when:

> Another poor man sent for him
> And he began to grieve.
> "I have no rest, nor joy, nor peace,
> For people die and die"
> And after cried he, "God forgive!
> My body spake, not I!"

The old priest intends to go visit the home of a dying man, but despite his good intentions, he is overcome by fatigue and falls asleep. When he awakes, he hurries to the dying man's house and is ashamed to discover that he's arrived too late to administer the last rites. But then, to his amazement, the newly widowed wife thanks him for coming earlier in the evening. He then realizes:

> "He who hath made the night of stars
> For souls, who tire and bleed,
> Sent one of his great angels down
> To help me in my need.
> He who is wrapped in purple robes,
> With planets in his care,
> Had pity on the least of these
> Asleep upon a chair."

God gives to those who are charitable, providing wealth, energy, and also joy. Chroniclers relate that Saint Ninian, the first Christian among the Picts, was "happy beyond measure." The secret of his unquenchable cheer was simply this: he gave clothing to those who had none, visited prisoners, and gave food to the hungry and drink to the thirsty. He did exactly what Jesus described as service to "the least of these"—and God recompensed him with continual joy.

The Celtic Christians not only practiced personal kindness, but they also worked to right larger wrongs. They had learned from the example set by their brothers and sisters in Egypt to care about justice.

The travelers who wrote the *Lives of the Desert Fathers* tell of their visit to the monastic community at Arsinoe, where there was "an enormous community numbering about ten thousand monks." This community sustained "a considerable rural economy" by pooling all the harvest from the monks' gardens. Then, "they provided this grain for the relief of the poor, so that there was nobody in that district who was destitute any longer. Indeed, grain was even sent to the poor of Alexandria." This practice was not unique to that monastery; the travelers explained that all the Desert Fathers and Mothers shared "this form of stewardship" and together "they dispatch whole shiploads of wheat and clothing to Alexandria for the poor, because it is rare for anyone in need to be found living near the monasteries."

Always eager to keep up with the Copts in spiritual endeavors, Celtic monks and nuns also established their communities as centers of generosity. By their practical example of kindness and justice, the early Irish and Scottish abbeys set a pattern for the entire society, modeling a standard of neighborly assistance that balanced the cruelties of the Dark Ages.

In the twenty-first century, a band of spiritually motivated Irish rock stars are still living out the spirit of Celtic generosity and justice. They have spearheaded efforts to share wealth and assist others on a global scale through the One Campaign, an "international, nonpartisan, nonprofit organization which aims to increase government funding for and effectiveness of international aid programs." Named after the song "One" by U2, the campaign is supported by politicians, including former president Bill Clinton, and by world religious leaders, including Archbishop Desmond Tutu of South Africa. The campaign has enabled 34 million African school children to receive life-saving drugs. (You can read more about U2's musical journey in the previous chapter).

Break Down the Walls
People in Need

After Mother Teresa became famous for her work with the sick and dying of Calcutta, people wrote her asking to come and serve with the Sisters of Charity. She responded, "Find your own Calcutta."

We are all near to people in need. But we some-times find ways to excuse ourselves—to justify inac-tion—when it comes to serving others. We may protest, "I'm too busy, too poor, too tired." Or we may excuse ourselves by saying, "That's not something I'm called to." And yet we want to serve Jesus, who appears as "the least of these, my brothers and sisters" who are hungry, thirsty, and sick. Deep in our hearts, we do long to be part of that healing stream of God's love pouring into the world.

But we do not nurture these longings for various rea-sons. Unfortunately, expenditures of time or effort do not always result in the benefits we intend. The problems in the world seem too big for our meager efforts to make any difference.

Too often, we reduce the concept of charity to sim-ply throwing money or material possessions at a prob-lem. Sometimes, in the midst of an urgent crisis, for example, that may be exactly what is needed. Other times, however, what's needed may be something quite different: someone to listen, possibly, or someone to teach and affirm. If we categorize our altruism into three categories, we may gain new insights into the ways we can make a difference in our world.

The first category—relief—is the simplest. It's the immediate aid given for very specific and concrete needs. Brigid giving the sword to the beggar and vol-unteers giving food in soup-lines are examples of this.

Relief is especially helpful after large-scale disasters, such as tsunamis, hurricanes, and floods.

The second category—empowerment—allows individuals to improve their situations by providing education, resources, or start-up capital, enabling the recipients to gain employment or begin their own small business. The increase of farmer Nesan's herd fits in this model, and in our own age, the program Jobs for Life gives homeless and formerly incarcerated people the job skills, interview techniques, and other talents needed to find employment.

And third, development transforms entire communities so that all members have access to employment or business ownership, so that no one is without a job and everyone has just wages. George MacLeod developed jobs for unemployed Glasgow workers when he re-established the Iona Community. Likewise, the monasteries of the Celts transformed the economies of entire kingdoms, providing work and food for all who needed them.

How can you make a difference? Where can you use your creativity and other resources to change the world?

Jesus told us to treat others the way we would want to be treated. This means we must see ourselves in each other; we must knock down the walls that seem to divide us from those in need. We are kidding ourselves, anyway, if we think the line between "us" and "them" is anything but tenuous. The day before writing this chapter, I stood on the "provider" side of a local food program, serving "clients" defined as "poor and needy." I was startled to discover that five of these people were friends I knew from my jobs or from civic organizations. Experiences like this illustrate how economic changes are removing distinctions between the middle class and the poor. One government decision to cut costs could place any of us on the receiving side of the local food program—and that could happen tomorrow.

More than ever, we need to share our gifts and talents with others. When we do so, Christ-within-us breaks bread with Christ-in-our-neighbors.

Your neighbor is thirsty. Give God a drink.

The stranger outside your door is lonely. Invite God into your home.

> *A shade art thou in the heat.*
> *A shelter art thou in the cold.*
> *Eyes art thou to the blind.*
> *A staff art thou to the pilgrim.*
> *An island art thou at sea.*
> *A fortress art thou on land.*
> *A well art thou in the desert.*
> *Health art thou to the ailing.*
> —*prayer for a young woman from the* Carmina Gadelica

In the Gospels, Jesus identifies himself with the outcast, the homeless, the marginalized. The Celtic Christians knew that true hospitality means we open the doors of both our hearts and our homes—and when we let others inside, we welcome Christ.

15
Uncharted Seas
Life's Pilgrimage

Others went out on the sea in ships. . . .
They mounted up to the heavens
and went down to the depths;
in their peril their courage melted away.
They reeled and staggered like drunken men;
they were at their wits' end.
Then they cried out to the Lord in their trouble,
and he brought them out of their distress.
He stilled the storm to a whisper;
the waves of the sea were hushed.
They were glad when it grew calm,
and he guided them to their desired haven.
Psalm 107:23–30

They were aliens and strangers on earth . . .
they were looking for a better country—a heavenly one.
Therefore God is not ashamed to be called their God,
for he has prepared a city for them.
Hebrews 11:13–16

Water from an Ancient Well

In May of 1976, adventurer Tim Severin and two fellow sailors found themselves in a truly frightening place: they were tossed up and down by tremendous Atlantic waves, far from land, inside a thirty-foot boat made of leather stitched over a wooden frame.

Severin was re-creating the voyage of the Irish Saint Brendan who—according to ancient manuscripts—around the year 575 sailed thousands of miles across the North Atlantic to reach a new world. The legends say that Brendan and his companions were delighted by this undiscovered country, but God told them not to stay there because their presence would spoil it. Many scholars, however, have doubted that Brendan's voyage was a historical event; they argued that a leather *curragh* boat could not hold up in a voyage through rough open seas.

So as the waves pounded against the sewn hides and the boat's frame twisted and creaked, Severin and his mates hoped desperately that their faith in a medieval manuscript—and in a boat made according to that text—would be justified.

Their little leather boat—named *The Brendan*—did hold up to the challenge. The voyage had harrowing moments, but Severin and his crew proved that a crossing from Ireland to Newfoundland was indeed possible. In fact, the places and stages of their adventure correlated perfectly with the ancient legends of Brendan's journey.

The man known as Brendan the Voyager inspired these modern adventurers to undertake this dangerous

UNCHARTED SEAS

voyage. But what inspired that holy monk himself to leave home at the close of the sixth century and take off across vast and unknown waters?

According to the ancient account, Brendan was "engaged in spiritual warfare in a place which is called Brendan's 'Meadow of Miracles,'" when a fellow monk named Barinthus returned from a lengthy sea voyage and regaled Brendan with tales of having visited "the Island of Delights," a hitherto unknown Eden-like land. Brendan straightaway selected seven monks, shut them in a prayer room with him, and told them, "My most beloved fellow-warriors, I look to you for advice and help, for my heart and thoughts are united in a single desire. I have resolved in my heart, if only it be God's will, to seek that Promised Land, of which St. Barinthus has spoken. How does that seem to you, and what advice do you wish to give me?"

His fellow monks were all equally excited to undertake the voyage.

Their enthusiasm is predictable, for the Celtic Christians were pilgrim people; their faith was not a search for security but an adventurous quest. As in many other areas of spiritual life, their pagan ancestors inspired them with stories and a spirit of courageous curiosity.

The ancient Irish knew that geese flew away from the west side of their island, and regularly returned from that same direction. "Surely," they thought, "there must be land in that direction." Over the years, brave sailors headed off toward the sunset, seeking the fabled Western Islands. These sailors' tales were called Immrama (the Gaelic word for "voyage"), exciting accounts of bold seamen's voyages to the West, seeking the Land of the Blessed.

One of the earliest Immram tales, "The Voyage of Bran," tells how a woman of the Sidhe told Bran about the Isle of the Blessed, a land full of light and perpetual joy, without sorrow, sickness, or death. Aided by the Sea God, Bran and his companions reached this paradise. They stayed there for many years, although to them, it seemed only a year. (We hear echoes here of Homer's tale of the Greek sea-faring hero, Odysseus.) When Bran and his companions returned home, the first of the crew to set foot on shore turned to ashes. Bran then related his story, copied it down in Ogham, and sailed away, never to be heard of again.

The Celtic Christians saw the parallels between Bran and Brendan; the wild geese flying westward still inspired them with a longing for adventure. For them, the Holy Spirit was *Ah Geadh-Glas*, the Wild Goose, one of those same strong fowls that fly in from who-knows-where, and then embark in formation for equally unknown distant destinations. The wild geese are like the wind of the Holy Spirit who "blows where it chooses, and you hear the sound of it, but you do not know where it comes from or where it goes" (John 3:8).

In common parlance a "wild goose chase" is a waste of time—but not if the goose is the Divine Spirit! For the Celts, the pursuit of God made life a grand exploration.

David Adam explains in his book titled *The Open Gate*, "As long as we are alive, we are on the move. To become static is to stagnate and die. It is necessary for all living things to move and grow and change. Life is meant to be an adventure."

For some Celtic saints, pilgrimage took the form of extreme adventure. The hardiest spiritual athletes undertook the White Martyrdom, a color chosen because, to quote Thomas Cahill, "they . . . sailed into the white sky of morning, into the unknown, never to return." These daring souls set their curraghs into the ocean and cast loose the rudder, asking Providence to direct their little leather vessels and land them where-and-when God chose.

Of course, the desire for pilgrimage neither began nor ended with the Celtic Christians. Cintra Pemberton in her book *Soulfaring* writes:

> Deeply religious people are pilgrim people; that is, they are always on the move, on an interior if not a literal journey, always seeking that which will draw them closer to their God, seeking that which is Holy. The tradition of pilgrimage is thus as old as humanity and is to be found among people of all faiths and all belief systems.

Pilgrimage takes place on two levels: inward and outward. As Martin and Nigel Palmer explain in *The Spiritual*

Water from an Ancient Well

Traveler, "Exploring a sacred place involves two journeys—physical and metaphysical—running side-by-side." One cannot embark on a physical voyage and assume that geographical relocation will lead to illumination. The pilgrim must prepare her soul for travel as much as her body. Phil Cousineau, in *The Art of Pilgrimage*, reminds us, "What matters most on your journey is how deeply you see, how attentively you hear, how richly the encounters are felt in your heart and soul."

The Celts regarded the entire world as sacred (see chapter 7, especially on Erigena's panentheist theology). Poet Elizabeth Browning writes: "Earth is crammed with heaven and every bush aflame with God." So you may well ask, "Why bother to travel in search of sacredness? Can't I find it in my backyard?"

Daniel Taylor, in his book *In Search of Sacred Places*, writes, "Most religions . . . teach that God is available everywhere. Why then should I go to Iona to find God rather than my bedroom closet?" He answers his question: "God is not any more, or less, on Iona than in my garage. And yet no one has reported an intense religious experience in my garage, and many have done so after visiting Iona." He adds, "If we are looking for gold, we listen when someone tells us where they've found gold. If we are looking for God, we listen when someone reports to have felt God close in a certain place."

Universal religious intuition, confirmed by the Hebrew scriptures, suggests a "both-and" rather than "either-or" solution to this question. The Divine Presence is everywhere (see Psalm 139), and yet mortals can *experience* that Presence more keenly in certain places than they would in ordinary settings. For instance, in Genesis 28 the patriarch Jacob flees from his brother Esau, traveling from Beersheba (the southernmost point of modern-day Israel) to Haran (in Syria, north of modern-day Israel). On his long trek, he stops and sleeps at "a certain place." There, "he had a dream in which he saw a stairway resting on the earth, with its top reaching to heaven, and the angels of God were ascending and descending on it" (Genesis 28:12). When Joseph awoke the next day, he declared, "Surely the Lord is in this place. . . . How awesome is this place! This is none other than the House of God; this is the gate of heaven." He then erected a standing stone and renamed the site "Bethel," which means "House of God."

The Celts regarded places of God's presence as "thin places" like Bethel, where the boundary that divides mundane physical existence from spiritual realities stretches to the point that it becomes transparent. At such places, those of us who live in this world can intersect with the invisible supernatural realm.

Natural settings are often thin places. Water may mark spiritual thresholds because water sustains life, can take life, and confuses our ability to see objects clearly. Caves seem like entrances to other realms, to below-worlds, and grottoes and caverns served as haunts for druids, hermits, and Christian ascetics. Hills and mountains lead the mind upward toward heaven, and their tops become lost in the mists; hence they become "stairways to heaven" and places of Divine revelation. (God delivered the Ten Commandments atop the towering heights of Mount Sinai, and Jesus ascended a mountain for his Transfiguration.) Ancient stone monuments—standing stones, dolmens, and monoliths—also attain holy and mysterious status; their origins forgotten, they became known as haunts for the Sidhe (spirits driven underground, the faery folk).

Thousands of years of tradition hallowed these sacred places in the Celtic lands. Gaelic people arriving in the British Isles around 500 BCE adapted already ancient thin places built by Neolithic peoples to their own use; after them, came the Christian saints and monks who built churches and adopted older holy wells as places to worship Christ; early medieval chapels were often built adjacent to (or even within) far more ancient standing-stone circles. Likewise, the ancient stones are commonly paired with holy wells. If you are visiting a sacred site in Ireland, Scotland, or Wales, look around carefully and you may be rewarded by finding Neolithic monument stones, a church building, and a holy well—all in close proximity. This is a thin place going back over a hundred generations. Imagine the prayers the stones and earth of such a place have heard, from the Stone Age until now.

The Glastonbury Tor and adjacent Chalice Well in southern England are good examples of the "double coding" of Celtic sacred sites. (Double coding is the use of one object to speak to different audiences in different ways.) The Tor is a large elongated hill, with its sides long ago worked to form a great labyrinth. For the Celts in druidic times, the Tor served as entrance to the underworld, and the nearby well—its waters turned red by iron oxide—was the menstrual blood of the Goddess. Glastonbury has been connected to Avalon of Arthurian legend, and the Tor is rumored to have been the hiding place of the Cauldron of Plenty.

Later legends say that the Tor was the site of the first church in Britain, founded by Joseph of Arimathea along with Lazarus, Mary and Martha, and Mary Magdalene. According to some tales, Joseph arrived at the hill and established a Christian community adjacent to the druid fellowship already there, and both faiths coexisted peacefully in that location. This tradition also says that Joseph brought with him the cup of the last supper (the Holy Grail), and that he put that holy relic in the Chalice Well, which is why it now runs red with the blood of Christ. Today, pagans and Christians both regard Glastonbury as an amazing thin place.

After the gospel took root in Celtic lands, pilgrims traveled to places associated with the missionaries and founders of faith. Medieval churchmen established Saint David's on the tip of the Pembrokeshire Peninsula in Wales as a favorite destination for pilgrims when the Church decreed that two pilgrimages to Saint David's equaled one to Rome, and three visits to Saint David's equaled a pilgrimage to Jerusalem.

Pilgrims today also venerate Croagh Patrick in County Mayo, Ireland. Each year, some 15,000 pilgrims ascend the mountain where the patron saint of Ireland went to fast and pray. On Reek Sunday (the Sunday nearest the Summer Solstice), some dedicated pilgrims risk hypothermia and wounds by climbing the mount barefoot.

Followers of Jesus in all ages have honored Jerusalem, the place of Christ's death and resurrection, as a pilgrimage site. Tragically, disputes over the Holy City led to centuries of bitter warfare between Christians and Muslims. But for centuries before the Crusades, Islam welcomed Christians on journeys to the Holy Land.

The trek from the British Isles to Jerusalem was long, difficult, and expensive, and few achieved that goal in the Dark Ages. Three who did make the journey were saints David, Padarn, and Teilo, all from Wales.

According to a medieval chronicler, they entered a great church in Jerusalem, and in the front of that sanctuary, they found three chairs. Two chairs were splendidly gilded, while the third was of plain wood. David and Padarn chose the ornate chairs, but Teilo chose the plain chair. A priest then explained that it was a test, and the chair Teilo sat in had been used by Christ himself. Teilo's choice signified that God would use him to be an outstanding teacher of the gospel.

The Celtic tradition provides numerous other models for spiritual pilgrimage: short trips to local shrines and holy wells, longer pilgrimages to sites associated with the great saints, dangerous journeys to the Holy Land, and for the bravest adventurers, the White Martyrdom. Brendan's quest for the Holy took him all the way from Ireland to the shores of North America, nine centuries before Columbus. Yet these voyages still fell short of the pilgrims' ultimate goal.

Perhaps one defining mark of a saint is the recognition that no place on this Earth is truly home. All of life is a pilgrimage, a journey toward the goal that lies beyond mortal existence. Ultimately, believers desire the sight of God, not dimly but face-to-face (1 Corinthians 13:12). However profound or life-changing earthly journeys may be, they are just a foretaste of the longed-for Divine union that still lies ahead.

All the Celtic saints' biographies dwell on their deaths: final actions, final words, and the events of their final moments merit telling in exquisite detail. This is not because the chroniclers were morbid or obsessed with death; far from it. Instead, they knew that the narrative of a believer's life would be incomplete and disappointing if the ending were not a crescendo, an assurance that the pilgrim had reached the far shore at last.

The Miracles of Bishop Nynia recounts the life of Scotland's first Christian missionary and then details the glory of his death. Ninian, who had suffered from a painful wasting illness at the end of his life, said before he died, "The potter's kiln shakes the pots with the force of the flame, but cruel burdens are the trials of just people. I should like to suffer dissolution and see Christ face to face."

Ninian's biographer then recounts what the saint experienced in the moments after death:

> He was immediately surrounded by the shining host, and now blazing bright in snow-white vestment, like phosphorous in the sky, he was carried in angel arms beyond the stars of heaven. Passing through the companies of the saints and the everlasting hosts, he rejoiced to visit the inner-most shrine of the King throned on high. He clearly perceived, united as he was with the celestial hosts in the halls of heaven, the glory of the Trinity, the hymns of gladness, together with the supreme denizens of the Holy City on high.

As Ninian's journey reached its triumphant end, the reader is encouraged to follow her own pilgrimage with courage and joy.

Solvitur Ambulando
Following the Right Track

The ancient Celts gave us varying approaches to pilgrimage, and these offer twenty-first-century pilgrims a diverse itinerary of possible adventures. Journeys of the soul may take days, months, even years before the traveler finds his resting place, while other spiritual journeys can be taken in a matter of hours, just outside the pilgrim's door.

Saint Augustine of Hippo coined the phrase "*solvitur ambulando*," which means, "it is solved by walking." The Celts and Augustine had their disagreements, but on this point they certainly agreed. As Nigel Pennick writes:

> To the Celtic saints, the simple everyday necessity of walking along a road was a spiritual act. . . . Being on the right track is a metaphor for the pilgrim's journey to paradise and the ancient Celtic track ways reflect this spiritual meaning in the material world.

If your mind is troubled, a brisk stroll can restore focus and calm. A walk through crowded urban sidewalks and alleys can, of course, be unnerving; there's little time to reflect if you must dodge frenzied human traffic. But even major metropolitan areas have parks, greenbelts, and recreation areas that invite more relaxed saunters.

Walking briskly, forty-five minutes to an hour each day, is a practical and helpful practice for staying positive. Try to walk along vegetation, on paths or sidewalks that demand little attention in terms of direction. Begin by consciously praying for people and causes, and then on the return leg of the walk, you can settle into a sense of "now-ness." Forgetting troubles of the past and concerns for the future, laying aside the cares and duties that await you at home, simply enjoy the air on your face, the sky above your head, the light that shows you the world as you pass. Such walking meditation frees you from the demands of your ego, even from a sense of self. When you return and pick up your life again, you will often find you perceive life from a perspective of Divine clarity. Truly, *solvitur ambulando.*

Labyrinths
Microcosms of Life's Journey

Some folks liken life to a maze, but a labyrinth may be a better metaphor. Labyrinths are devices for walking meditation, designed for peacefulness and spiritual encounter. Unlike a maze, which is designed to trap or confuse the walker, a labyrinth will always lead to the center and then back out again. At times, the rambler may feel disoriented, as the labyrinth appears to bring her close to the center and then heads away again, but that is also part of the message: though she may wander, the walker is never lost.

The earliest known depiction of a labyrinth is from Pontevedra, Spain, in Galicia, what was once a Celtic province. The British Isles also have several ancient labyrinth portrayals that date to Celtic times: one in Cornwall near Tintagel and one on the slopes of Glastonbury Tor. Legends associate the first site with King Arthur's birth and the latter with his place of rest.

Labyrinths are designed to be microcosms of life's journey, models of spiritual pilgrimage. As a pilgrimage, a labyrinth walk typically consists of three stages: releasing your concerns on the inward walk, connecting with God at the center, and preparing for service while heading back out toward ordinary space. (To find a labyrinth near you, go to the World-Wide Labyrinth Locator: labyrinthlocator.com).

Sacred Spots
Finding Your Own Thin Place

Spiritual seekers long ago recognized that certain natural sites were thin places where they glimpsed God's presence. This is true not only in the British Isles but throughout the world. Native people in North America recognized many sacred sites and marked them with petroglyphs. These sites existed on their own before humans came along and designated them as places of revelation—so why shouldn't you expect to find your own thin place where you live?

As I mentioned in chapter 5, I have my own special meditation place, an enormous rock I have dubbed "Aslan's Throne." It's several miles from my house just off a hiking trail overlooking a creek, a quiet place for meditation and prayer amid the pines. I don't know that anyone else besides me considers this to be a thin place, but for me, it definitely seems so.

Who knows what sacred spots may wait for discovery on the trails you walk? For that matter, you might also identify certain stages on your life journey as thin places where God revealed God's self to you. If you map out your spiritual pilgrimage on a large sheet of unlined paper, from birth to now, making notes (drawings perhaps) of special places, people, and events that were important to you along the way, you may gain a better sense of your own life's labyrinth.

Don't Just Travel
Go on a Pilgrimage

If you are blessed with the time and finances, a traveling pilgrimage to the same holy places that pilgrims have journeyed to for more than a thousand years can be an amazing spiritual adventure. Joan Halifax, in her book *A Fruitful Darkness*, writes, "Everybody has a [familiar] geography. . . . That is why we travel to far-off places. Whether we know it or not, we need to renew ourselves in territories that are fresh and wild. We need to come home through the body of alien lands."

Christians from around the world still travel to the original Holy Land—Israel—and especially Jerusalem. Although scarred by violence and marred by tackiness, the locations where Jesus and the Prophets walked still inspire. The foremost Christian holy site is the Church of the Holy Sepulcher, containing the place of Jesus' crucifixion and the site of the Empty Tomb. (Scholars argue the authenticity of both, but Christian pilgrims have trekked to these same spots since the early fourth century.) If you do visit the Holy Land, don't forget to spend time with the "living temple"—Christians who have worshiped Jesus in the land of his birth since the first century. They struggle to hold their place, but indigenous Christians in the Holy Land have a powerful story to tell and an extremely ancient set of traditions to share.

I also highly recommend traveling to "the other Holy Land," the British Isles where Patrick, Brigid, and Columba ministered. Pilgrims still embark for the shores of the holy island of Iona, seeking a touch from God—and the journey continues to reward them. There, amid ancient ruins and the graves of Scotland's medieval kings, stands a lovely reconstructed Abbey and—more important— a vibrant community of faith that offers deep worship experiences. The pilgrim's city of St. David's in Wales is also a rewarding place. Walking along the Pembrokeshire Path, the modern pilgrim sees dramatic views of cliffs, bracken, and ocean, along with occasional ruins from Neolithic, Iron Age, and Christian eras. The Cathedral of Saint David is a splendid piece of Middle Ages architecture and the home for a vibrant community of faith.

Then there is the Way of Saint James, the Camino

de Santiago de Compostela, in Galicia, northwest Spain. This is an ancient Celtic region, the homeland, Irish myth claims, of the Milesians, ancestors of today's Irish. The walk to the Cathedral of Saint James is the most-trod pilgrim's path in today's world.

If you do venture forth on a traveling pilgrimage, you'll need to do a few things to distinguish it from a mere sightseeing trip. A pilgrimage takes time, especially at destination points. Plan your trip so you can spend leisurely moments, at your own pace and agenda, at sacred destinations. If you can, arrive early or stay late. Leave time to pray and to be still, to listen and to feel. God may speak to you through the place itself or through fellow pilgrims. I also like to take an envelope full of prayer requests from my acquaintances, and then open the envelope, read the requests, and pray for my far-away friends at sacred sites.

Mementos of the journey can also be powerful reminders of your experience, relics more meaningful than those sold at the nearest tourist store. Traditionally, shells were symbols of pilgrimage, for they proved the pilgrim had made it across the ocean and back. On my desk, I have a much-treasured reminder of my time at Iona, a piece of bright-green rock from Columba's Bay. These small, tactile objects allow us to bring our journey home with us, so that in the midst of our ordinary lives, sitting in our offices or living rooms, we can access once again a small piece of the spiritual experience.

Of course, God is not bound to our desires, and so a

pilgrimage may not turn out to be what you expected. You may face troubles and hardships; plans may have to change, and desires go unfulfilled. The site you think will bring a grand epiphany might turn out to be a disappointment . . . but on the other hand, a place where you had no expectation might prove to hold the Holy Grail. Be open to God meeting you wherever and however God will. Phil Cousineau warns, "If the journey you have chosen is indeed a pilgrimage, a soulful journey, it will be rigorous. Ancient wisdom suggests if you aren't trembling as you approach the sacred, it isn't the real thing. The sacred . . . evokes emotion and commotion."

The Final Adventure
Death

Many of the great saints kept human skulls in their places of study. They weren't being morbid. Instead, these skulls were reminders that they each held a guaranteed ticket for the grandest adventure of all. Death waits for all of us—we carry that reality in our flesh and bones—but that fact need not fill us with dread and dismay. Instead, if we follow the example of the ancient saints, we will think of death as the greatest adventure of all.

When a young reporter asked George MacLeod, the venerable elder minister of his time, what he thought of death, he replied, "On the whole, I'm in favor of it." If you are a follower of Jesus, death is not something frightening, and it is not "the end." Jesus calls us his friends, and he promises that he has prepared wonderful places for us, places where we will know the joy of God's presence in its fullness.

The culmination of mortal life, as C. S. Lewis wrote at the very end of his Narnia tales, is "Chapter One of the Great Story, which no one on earth has read: which goes on forever: in which every chapter is better than the one before." So dare to venture into uncharted seas. Like the mariner saints, embrace life as a pilgrimage. Journey fearlessly, with joy and excitement.

Plunge into the same water the ancient Celts explored. The God of all Compassion awaits you on the other side.

> *See that you be at peace among yourselves,*
> *my children, and love one another.*
> *Follow the example of good men of old,*
> *and God will comfort you and help you,*
> *both in this world*
> *and in the world which is to come.*
> *—Saint Columba*

The written account of St. Brendan's voyage is filled with amazing details that give credence to the story (descriptions of icebergs and actual islands to the west), as well as fantastical events that stretch the reader's credulity as much as any article in the National Enquirer. *Ancient and medieval hagiography was not strictly factual in the modern sense of the world, however; it often used symbolic narrative passages to reveal deeper spiritual truths. Brendan's story, with its tales of whales and adventures and spiritual challenge, inspires us to encounter the unknown with open hearts. It teaches us that curiosity and courage are important aspects of the spiritual life.*

Appendix

How to Make a Saint Brigid's Cross

According to legend, Saint Brigid began the custom of hand-weaving crosses from natural materials. Today, Irish believers still make fresh Brigid's crosses each year to protect their homes, weaving them on February 1, her saint's day.

Traditionally Brigid's crosses are made of wheat or freshly cut river reeds. For your own project, you can buy weaver's wheat at a craft store, then boil it in water and let it soak overnight—or for a far more simple project, use craft pipe cleaners or plastic straws. If you are fortunate to live near a river, cut reeds and soak them in lukewarm water until you begin your project.

The directions that follow may seem complex, but once you've mastered them, the procedure is simple and relaxing.

1. Cut 16 even-length pieces of wheat, each approximately 11 inches long, and lay them on a table in front of you. I also like to have a couple of extra pieces ready if one breaks—but keep those on the side; you could get confused if you have more than 16 pieces in the pile.

You might want to get small spring-loaded clothes pins, to hold the folded ends together at each step. I've heard of using rubber bands for the same purpose, but I find those require more dexterity than I have.

2. Place the first piece on the table in front of you, heading vertically away from you.

3. Take a second piece of straw and fold it in half, over and under the middle of the first piece, heading horizontally off to your right. You now have a cross that is missing the left arm.

4. Holding it where the pieces intersect, rotate the cross in front of you one-quarter turn (90 degrees) counterclockwise. The long piece is now horizontal and the folded-in-half piece is aiming vertically away from you.

5. Take the third piece of straw, fold it in half, and place it over the center folded-in-half straw, and above the long single piece, with the ends pointing horizontally to your right. Looking at it, you now have a cross that's missing the bottom vertical piece.

6. Now repeat, moving the whole assembly counterclockwise 90 degrees, then placing the next folded piece over the center and atop the other pieces, going to your right horizontally.

7. Continue doing the same maneuver until you have used up all your pieces. At that point, you should have four pieces (eight ends) going in each direction.

8. Pull all the pieces (all four directions) to tighten-up the middle square.

9. Using natural cordage or raffia, tie-off the four cross-arms about 1 inch from the end.

10. Let it dry overnight. You may wish to put a few spots of white glue in the center for more permanence.

11. Dedicate your cross with a prayer and hang it in your home or workplace. Traditionally, St. Brigid's crosses are placed over doors for protection and blessing as you come and go.

Chapter Notes

Introduction

The prayer at the end is from *Earth Afire with God: Celtic Prayers for Ordinary Life* (Anamchara Books, 2011). This book is a collection of both ancient prayers in modern language, as well as prayers written from a Celtic perspective by modern spiritual seekers.

Chapter 1

Rumi's poem "The Reed Flute Song" is from Coleman Barks, *The Essential Rumi* (Castle, 1997).

General information on the ancient Celts is from Juliette Wood's visually sumptuous book, *The Celts: Life, Myth and Art* (Barnes & Noble, 2004), as well as Stephen Allen's *Celtic Warrior: 300 BC–AD 100* (Osprey Books, 2001).

My source on things druidic is Peter Berresford Ellis's work *The Druids* (Eerdmans, 2004).

Information on Glastonbury and its ancient Christian heritage is from *King Arthur's Avalon: the Story of Glastonbury*, by Geoffrey Ashe (Fontana, 1973).

For Paul's letter to the Galatians, the story of St. Patrick, and an overview of Celtic Christianity in general, see Thomas Cahill's acclaimed work, *How the Irish Saved Civilization: The Untold Story of Ireland's Heroic Role from the Fall of Rome to the Rise of Medieval Europe* (Doubleday, 1996).

Regarding the transition from paganism to Christianity, see Geoffrey Moorhouse's delightful book *Sun Dancing: A Vision of Medieval Ireland* (Harcourt Brace, 1997).

The information on Egyptian-Celtic connections came from "The Egyptian Connection," by William Dalrymple in *The New York Review of Books*, Volume 55, Number 16, October 23, 2008. Dalrymple's article cites three further sources on that topic.

For Columbanus's life and influence, see Tomas Fiach, *Columbanus in His Own Words* (Veritas, 1974).

Chapter 2

The best source for all things related to Brigid is *Brigid of the Gael: A Guide for the Study of Saint Brigid of Kildare*, by Conrad Bladey (Hutman Productions, 2009).

Excerpts from Columbanus's *Sermon, The Broom of Devotion*, and *Food for the Soul* are all taken from *The Classics of Western Spirituality: Celtic Spirituality*, by Oliver Davies (Paulist Press, 1999). This collection of translated primary documents is an invaluable source of information for those pursuing Celtic studies.

Quotes from Bernard of Clairvaux are from the modern-language version by Anamchara Books (2011).

CHAPTER NOTES

The quote from Julian of Norwich is from Ellyn Sanna's modern-language version of Julian's Showings, *All Shall Be Well* (Anamchara Books, 2011). This book overflows with Julian's confidence in the Divine Lover.

A practical and accessible devotional on loving God is *Passion for Jesus: Perfecting Extravagant Love for God*, by Mike Bickle (Creation House, 1994).

Chapter 3

You can follow Andy Rogers's adventures playing "Be Thou My Vision" and other Celtic tunes at his website, www.andyrogersmusic.com. From there you can link to his blog, download music, and watch videos.

Alexander Carmichael's amazing collection of old Scots oral traditions, the *Carmina Gadelica*, is available online at this URL: www.sacred-texts.com/neu/celt/cg1/index.htm, or in print version as *Carmina Gadelica: Hymns and Incantations from the Gaelic* (Floris Books, 2004). All entries are in both the English translation and in the lovely old Gaelic. Throughout this book, I have made frequent use of the modern versions of the *Carmina Gadelica* and other Celtic prayers found in *Earth Afire with God: Celtic Prayers for Ordinary Life* (Anamchara Books, 2011).

You'll find ideas on how to "mezuzah your universe" in Leonard Sweet's book of spirituality, *Learn to Dance the Soul Salsa* (Zondervan, 2000). Sweet is a prolific writer and a very creative Christian postmodern thinker.

The Chesterton quote is found in Dale Turner's *Different Seasons* (High Tide Press, 1998).

The delightful poem at the end of this chapter comes from a collection of similar offerings titled *Celtic Praise: A Book of Celtic Devotion, Daily Prayers and Blessings*, by Robert Van De Weyer (Nashville, Abingdon Press, 1998).

Chapter 4

Material on symbolism, ancient stone crosses, the roots of the wheel-cross pattern, and its association with the sun come from Jakob Streit's *Sun and Cross: From Megalithic Culture to Early Christianity in Ireland* (Floris Books, 2004).

Comments by C. S. Lewis are from *Mere Christianity* (MacMillan, 1960).

Theories of atonement are discussed at length in *Recovering the Scandal of the Cross: Atonement in New Testament & Contemporary Contexts*, by Joel B. Green and Mark D. Baker (Inter Varsity Press, 2000).

Observations on Anglo-Saxon views of the cross and a translation of "The Dream of the Rood" are from *The Classics of Western Spirituality: Anglo-Saxon Spirituality*, translated and introduced by Robert Boenig (Paulist Press, 2000). Like its companion piece, *Celtic Spirituality*, this is a must-have compilation of primary sources for students of ancient English Christianity.

For the contents of the ancient Iona library, see appendix in Thomas Owen Clancy's and Gilbert Márkus's

CHAPTER NOTES

Iona: the Earliest Poetry of a Celtic Monastery (Edinburgh University Press, 1995).

The Gospel of Nicodemus (Acts of Pilate) is found in *The Apocryphal New Testament: Being the Apocryphal Gospels, Acts, Epistles and Apocalypses with other Narratives and Fragments*, translated by Montague James Roads (Clarendon Press, 1969).

A thorough treatment of Christ's descent into Hell is *Christ the Conqueror of Hell: The Descent into Hades from and Orthodox Perspective*, by Archbishop Hilarion Alfeyev (Saint Vladimir's Seminary Press, 2009).

George Breed's *Embodying Spirit: The Inner Work of the Warrior* (iUniverse, 2004) is a whimsical and practical approach to spiritual life, based on a broad variety of world religious traditions.

More of Derek Flood's thoughts can be found on his blog, *The Rebel God*, www.therebelgod.com.

The prayer claiming the cross's protection is from *Earth Afire with God*, cited earlier.

Information on the sign of the cross comes from a website article, www.geocities.com/saintpeter_oshawa/articles-SignCross.html. Also, an article titled "Martin Luther on Making the Sign of the Cross," at www.angelfire.com/ny4/djw/lutherantheology.signofthecross.html.

Daily Light from the Celtic Saints, by Ray Simpson (Anamchara Books, 2013), consists of readings for each day of the year, arranged in sets of topics and incorporating an impressive knowledge of ancient Celtic Christianity.

Chapter 5

The Life of Merlin, by Geoffrey of Monmouth, is available online at www.sacred-texts.com/neu/eng/vm/vmeng.htm.

Accounts of Saint Anthony are from *Athanasius: The Life of Antony and the Letter to Marcellinus* (Paulist, 1980). I have chosen to use the more common form of the saint's name, spelling Anthony with a "th."

For accounts of desert hermits, I used *The Lives of the Desert Fathers* (Cistercian Publications, 1981).

Quotations by Thomas Merton come from *The Wisdom of the Desert* (New Directions, 1960).

The Life of St. Illtud (twelfth century) is online thanks to the Celtic Literature Collective at www.maryjones.us/ctexts/illtud.html.

Information about druidic forms of meditation comes from the online article "Shamanism in Gaelic Culture (or What Do We Call Our People?)," by Iain Mac and Saoir, part of The Clannada na Gadelica, a Gaelic culture education facility at www.clannada.org/culture_shamanism.php.

Richard Foster quotes are from *Celebration of Discipline* (Harper & Row, 1978).

Richard Rohr quotes are from *Everything Belongs: The Gift of Contemplative Prayer* (Crossroad, 2003).

CHAPTER NOTES

Chapter 6

For Saint Anthony, see *The Life of Anthony and the Letter to Marcellinus by Athansius, in the Classics of Western Spirituality* (Paulist Press, 1980)

For information on Irish monastic asceticism, read *Sun Dancing: A Vision of Medieval Ireland*, by Geoffrey Moorhouse (Harcourt Brace and Company, 1997).

Quotes from Dallas Willard, *The Spirit of the Disciplines: Understanding How God Changes Lives* (Harper & Row, 1988).

A fantastic daily devotional—genuine and deeply rooted—is *Celtic Daily Light: A Spiritual Journey through the Year*, by Ray Simpson (Kevin Mayhew, 2007). Others are *Celtic Daily Prayer*, by the Northumbria Community (Harper Collins, 2002), and *The Celtic Year: A Celebration of Celtic Christian Saints, Sites and Festivals*, by Shirley Toulson (Vega, 2002)

Chapter 7

Ninian's *Catechism* is from *Celtic Fire: An Anthology of Celtic Christian Literature*, by Robert Van de Weyer (Daron, Longman and Todd, 1990).

Taliesin's "Loves" is the modern-language version found in *Earth Afire with God*, cited previously.

Information on Erigena's theology comes from two sources: *The Voice of the Eagle: The Heart of Celtic Christianity*, by Christopher Bamford (Lindisfarne Books, 2000), and *Great Medieval Thinkers: John Scottus Eriugena,* by Deirdre Carabine (Oxford University Press, 2000).

Quotes from Julian of Norwich come from *Classics of Western Spirituality: Julian of Norwich Showings* (Paulist, 1978)

Information on the astronomical discoveries of the ancient Irish comes from *The Druids,* by Peter Berresford Ellis (Eerdmans, 1994).

For the ancient restoration of Britain's ecology, see *The Spiritual Traveler: England, Scotland, Wales,* by Martin Palmer and Nigel Palmer (Paulist, 2000).

Insights by J. Philip Newell come from his delightful book *Christ of the Celts: The Healing of Creation* (Jossey-Bass, 2008).

Chapter 8

The two stories of Columba—one about his horse, the other about a crane—come from *Life of Saint Columba, Founder of Hy. Written by Adamnan, Ninth Abbot of that Monastery,* ed. William Reeves. (Edinburgh: Edmonston and Douglas, 1874). This is available unabridged online at www.fordham.edu/halsall/basis/columba-e.html. I have retold the old accounts.

Stories of Saint Brigid (the boar and the fox) come from *Brigid of the Gael* (cited above).

The account of Ailbe and the wolf comes from Shirley Toulson, *The Celtic Year* (cited above). The book includes a nice illustration of Ailbe and his wolf-mother.

Chapter Notes

The legend of Tuan comes from *Celtic Myths and Legends*, by T. W. Rolleston (Dover, 1990).

Stories of the Egyptian snake-and-crocodile handlers come from the aforementioned *Lives of the Desert Fathers*.

The cat poem titled "Pangur Ban" can be found in many places and a wide variety of different translations. I took this one from the Fish Eaters website: www.fish-eaters.com/pangurban.html. The site also includes the original Gaelic text, which will give you more sense of the sound.

Anecdotes related to Francis of Assisi come from *The Lessons of Saint Francis: How to Bring Simplicity and Spirituality into Your Daily Life*, by John Michael Talbot and Steve Rabey (Penguin, 1998).

Return to Eden: A New Look at Old Relationships—Man, Animal, and God, by Dean Harrison (Out of Africa, 1998), is the fascinating, profound, and touching story of Dean and Prayeri Harrison's life together with large predators.

I found the prayer at the end of this chapter in *God's Creatures Great & Small: Prayers for our Pets and Other Animals*, by Judith A. Bauer (Regina Press, 2006).

Chapter 9

My fictionalized account of how John, Bishop of Wexham, healed a boy is based on Bede's *The Ecclesiastical History of the English People*.

WATER FROM AN ANCIENT WELL

Theological definitions for "miracle" are from *Touching the Supernatural World*, by Kenneth McIntosh (Mason Crest, 2005), and also from *God in the Dock: Essays on Theology and Ethics*, by C. S. Lewis (Eerdmans, 1970).

Columba's miracles are from *Life of Saint Columba, Founder of Hy. Written by Adamnan, Ninth Abbot of that Monastery*, ed. William Reeves (Edmonston and Douglas, 1874) and available online at *Medieval Sourcebook*, www.fordham.edu/halsall/basis/columba-e.html.

The encircling prayer is from *Earth Afire with God*, cited previously.

Kenton Sparks' remarks on the plausibility of miracles come from *God's Word in Human Words: An Evangelical Appropriation of Critical Biblical Scholarship* (Baker, 2008). Most of this book has nothing to do with the topic of this chapter, but useful remarks concerning miracles begin page 313.

"Medical Miracles Really Do Happen: Thousands of Cases Involving Seemingly Inexplicable Recoveries Have Been Reported by Doctors Around the World," by Larry Dossey, MD, is online at www.bottomlinesecrets.com/article.html?article_id=42254.

Finally, several useful chapters on miracles, prayer and visions are contained in *The Soul of Celtic Spirituality: In the Lives of Its Saints*, by Michael Mitton (Twenty-Third Publications, 1996).

CHAPTER NOTES

Chapter 10

The professor's testimony of seeing angels, along with many other anecdotal accounts of angelic "sightings," can be found in the author's book *Touching the Supernatural World*, cited above.

Accounts of angels and Columba are from *Daily Light from the Celtic Saints*, already cited.

The story of Cedd is from *The Soul of Celtic Spirituality.*

The Account of Saint Anthony is from Athanasius's *Life of Antony*, cited above.

C. S. Lewis's quote on dimensions comes again from *God in the Dock.*

Martin Rees quotes are from www.edge.org.

A recommended and thorough resource for spiritual warfare is Neil Anderson's *Spiritual Conflicts and Biblical Counseling* (Freedom in Christ Ministries, 1989).

Chapter 11

The story of Kevin's visit and the resuscitation of Kiernan are from *OrthodoxWiki*: "Kevin of Glendalough," orthodoxwiki. org/Kevin_of_Glendalough#Glendalough_Monastery.

Information on ring forts and women's roles in Celtic society is from *People of the Ancient World: The Ancient Celts*, by Patricia Calvert (Franklin Watts, 2005).

Notes on the symbolism of Celtic homes and

hospitality customs were found in *Kindling the Celtic Spirit*, by Mara Freeman (Harper Collins, 2000).

Citation regarding the druids' role in Celtic society is from *Celtic Myths and Legends*, by T. W. Rolleston (Dover, reprinted 1990).

Quotes on Trinitarian views of community and the definition of soul friend are from Mitton, *The Soul of Celtic Spirituality*, cited above.

Information on Queen Medb and *The Cattle Raid of Cooley* is in Cahill's *How the Irish Saved Civilization* (aforementioned).

Although he decried the practice, the historian Bede, who represented the Roman church, admitted in his accounts that there were married monks within Celtic monasteries in his time (the seventh century).

Notes on the physical shape of Irish communities and monasteries are from *Sun and Cross*, by Jakob Streit, cited above.

The information regarding possible Sanskrit origins of the Gaelic word "anamchara" is found under the chapter titled "Soul Friends" in Geoffrey Moorhouse's *Sun Dancing*, cited above.

Quotes regarding churches and perfectionism come from C. S. Lewis's delightful classic *The Screwtape Letters* (Macmillan, 1952).

Thoughts on St. Aidan and making friends "on the way" come from David Adam's *Flame in My Heart: St. Aidan for Today* (Morehouse Publishing, 1998).

Chapter Notes

Chapter 12

Quotes on the beauty of the Book of Kells are from *The Book of Kells,* by Bernard Meehan (Thames and Hudson, 1997).

Attestations to Celtic love for scripture are from *The Soul of Celtic Christianity,* by Michael Mitton and from *How the Irish Saved Civilization,* by Thomas Cahill (both previously cited).

Comments on scripture as story are from *Models for Scripture,* by John Goldingay (Eerdmans, 1994), and from *The Soul of Christianity,* by Huston Smith (Harper Collins, 2005).

Erigena's methods of interpretation are from *John Scottus Eriugena,* by Deirdre Carabine (aforementioned).

Notes on the Saxon translation of Psalm 137 are found in *Anglo-Saxon Christianity,* by Paul Cavill (previously cited).

Chapter 13

For a brief history of U2, see *Pop Rock: U2,* by Kenneth McIntosh (Mason Crest, 2008).

The story of Caedmon's miraculous singing talent comes from Bede's *Ecclesiastical History of the English People,* book IV, chapter 24.

Notes on Celtic visual arts, the mythical import of music and art in both paganism and Christianity, and the history of the Celtic harp are all found in *Kindling the Celtic Spirit,* by Mara Freeman (previously cited).

Description of the metal and jewelry work of the earliest Celts comes from chapter 1 of Sean O Duinn's excellent and scholarly work *Where Three Streams Meet: Celtic Spirituality* (Columba Press, 2006).

Readers intrigued by Celtic calligraphy and drawing will enjoy *Celtic Art: The Methods of Construction*, by George Bain (Dover, 1973).

Information on Irish high crosses comes from Hilary Richardson's *An Introduction to Irish High Crosses* (Mercier Press, 1990).

Steve Turner's book *Imagine: A Vision for Christians in the Arts* (Intervarsity Press, 2001) contains much inspiration and deep reflection on art and spirituality in the twenty-first century.

Chapter 14

The Brigid story from the Book of Lismore is again from *Brigid of the Gael*, cited above.

Kurt Neilson's book *Urban Iona: Celtic Hospitality in the City* (Morehouse Publishing, 2007) is a great example of ancient Celtic faith lived in the grit of modern life.

Information on Pelagius and George MacLeod are from *Listening to the Heartbeat of God* (Paulist Press, 1997), by J. Philip Newell, formerly warden of the Iona Community.

The story of Columba and Nesan is from *Daily Light from the Celtic Saints*, cited above.

"The Ballad of Father Gilligan" is from *W.B. Yeats: Selected Poems* (Random House, 1992).

The description of the Egyptian Fathers' and Mothers'

charity is in chapter 18 of *The Lives of the Desert Fathers*, cited above.

Chapter 15

The Brendan Voyage: A Leather Boat Tracks the Discovery of America by the Irish Sailor Saints, by Tim Severin (McGraw-Hill, 1978), is a rousing nonfiction adventure tale.

Details from *The Voyage of Brendan* are in the *Classics of Western Spirituality: Celtic Spirituality*, cited above.

Some great guidebooks for pilgrims to the Celtic lands are *Soulfaring: Celtic Pilgrimage Then and Now*, by Cintra Pemberton O.S.H. (Morehouse Publishing, Harrisburg PA, 1999); *Legends in the Landscape*, by Dara Ó Maoildhia (Aisling Publications, available at www.daramolloy. com/legends.html); and *The Spiritual Traveler: England, Scotland and Wales*, by Martin Palmer and Nigel Palmer (Hidden Spring, 2000.)

Sacred Wells: A Study in the History, Meaning and Mythology of Holy Wells & Waters, by Gary R. Varner (PublishAmerica, 2002), is the most complete book on this topic.

Acknowledgements

A large group of midwives helped birth this book. First, my parents—now part of that great host in the other realm—gave me a passion for reading and for our Celtic roots. My sister Joyce continues their tradition of loving me unconditionally and encouraging my dreams. My wife, Marsha, has been loving, forgiving, and supportive through more than a decade of my pursuing writing, a pursuit sometimes undertaken at the expense of other valuable things. Ellyn and Paul Sanna have been most precious friends and longtime supporters. The rest of the Anamchara crew, including Camden Flath, Sheila Stewart, and Russell Richardson, have all worked hard to see this book reach print. Rob Mullen plowed through the first half of the book, straightening out the writing. Craig Goodworth gave the whole rough draft a thorough, wise, and artistically informed critique that was invaluable in giving it cohesion. Caitlin Shideler and Lilly Weichberger also vetted the contents, adding helpful corrections and insights. Leonard Sweet, Father Richard Rohr, Ray Simpson, and Dara Molloy graciously offered their reviews. I'm sure there are others who helped in ways large and small, and I pray they will be kind as to forgive my omission if I have overlooked their names and contributions here. Finally, I am grateful to the One in whom I live and move and have my being, the High King of Heaven, my Lover, my All.

Index

WATER FROM AN ANCIENT WELL

INDEX

INDEX

INDEX

INDEX

INDEX

INDEX

WATER FROM AN ANCIENT WELL

wilderness: 21, 89, 94, 98, 104, 135, 157

Willard, Dallas: 118, 327

wind: 34, 57, 96, 298

wine: 169, 178, 193

Winifred, Saint: 176

Wink, Walter: 190

women: 49–50
    equality: 8, 17, 18, 226,
    231–232, 282–283

Word, the (see, Logos)

worship: 31, 40, 43, 58, 67, 73, 88, 132, 135–137, 231, 260, 261, 302, 311

Wright, N.T.: 257

yearning (see, longing)

Yeats, William Butler: 24, 287–288

yoga: 111

Made in the USA
San Bernardino, CA
13 May 2017